# SARTRE'S EXISTENTIALISM
# AND EARLY BUDDHISM

# SARTRE'S EXISTENTIALISM AND EARLY BUDDHISM

*A COMPARATIVE STUDY OF SELFLESSNESS THEORIES*

**Phra Medhidhammaporn**
**(Prayoon Mererk)**

BUDDHADHAMMA FOUNDATION
BANGKOK THAILAND

*First Published 1988*
*in*
*Bangkok Thailand*
*Second Edition*
*1995*


*ISBN 974–7890–43–7*

Publishers: Buddhadhamma Foundation,
87/126 Tesabahl Songkroh Rd., Lad Yao, Chatuchak, BANGKOK
THAILAND
Tel.: (66) (2) 589-9012
Fax : (66) (2) 954-4791

# PREFACE

The present work is a revised version of my doctoral thesis entitled *A Comparative Study of the Non-egological Treatments of Consciousness in Sartre's Philosophy and Early Buddhism*, which was submitted at the University of Delhi, India, in September 1985. The purpose of this study is to compare and contrast Sartre's doctrine of non-egology with the theory of selflessness (*anattā*) in Early (Theravāda) Buddhism. Since I embarked on this thesis I have entertained the wish that it would stimulate more interest in the comparative study of Buddhism and existentialism, and that my thesis would serve as a starting point for further research.

This thesis would not have been completed had it not been for the contribution and assistance of innumerable individuals. Although all of them cannot be acknowledged here, my sincere appreciation for their part is registered on these pages.

I would like to acknowledge with gratitude my indebtedness to Professor Margaret Chatterjee, Director of Indian Institute of Advanced Study, Simla, India, and Professor Mahesh Tiwary, University of Delhi, Delhi, India, for their noble guidance and invaluable suggestions at various stages of preparing the thesis.

I take this opportunity of making full acknowledgment of my gratitude to the Most Venerable Phra Thammahaviranuvat, Abbot of Wat Raikhing, Nakhorn Pathom, for granting me the scholarship to carry out this research project.

I would also like to thank the Buddhadhamma Foundation for taking on the republication of the work.

*Phra Medhidhammaporn*

# Abbreviations

| | |
|---|---|
| A. | Aṅguttara-Nikāya |
| AA. | Aṅguttara-Nikāya Aṭṭhakathā |
| Abhs. | Abhidhammatthasaṅgaha |
| BN. | Being and Nothingness |
| BPS. | Buddhist Publication Society |
| Brh. | Bṛhadāraṇyaka |
| Chand. | Chāndogya |
| CPR. | Critique of Pure Reason |
| D. | Dīgha-Nikāya |
| Dhp. | Dhammapada |
| Dhs. | Dhammasaṅganī |
| DhsA. | Dhammasaṅganī Aṭṭhakathā |
| Iti. | Itivuttaka |
| JPTS. | Journal of the Pali Text Society |
| Kvu. | Kathāvatthu |
| KvuA. | Kathāvatthu Aṭṭhakathā |
| M. | Majjhima-Nikāya |
| MA. | Majjhima-Nikāya Aṭṭhakathā |
| MK. | Mūlamādhyamakakārikā |
| Mand. | Māṇḍūkya |
| Miln. | Milindapañhā |
| Mund. | Muṇḍaka |
| PEW. | Philosophy East and West |
| PPR. | Philosophy and Phenomenological Research |
| PTS. | Pali Text Society |
| S. | Saṁyutta-Nikāya |
| SN. | Suttanipāta |
| Tait. | Taitirīya |
| TE. | The Transcendence of the Ego |
| Ud. | Udāna |
| Up. | Upaniṣad |
| Vism. | Visuddhimagga |

# Contents

# INTRODUCTION

There are at least three possibilities open to the student keen on comparing existentialism with Buddhism: (I) to make a comparative study of the basic concepts of existentialism with those of Buddhism, (2) to compare the basic concepts of any *one* existentialist philosopher with those of Buddhism, and (3) to present Buddhism in the existentialist perspective.[1] We are basically interested in the second possibility. The present work is an attempt to explore similarities and differences between Jean-Paul Sartre's philosophy and early Buddhism in regard to their non-egological treatments of consciousness *(viññāṇa)*. Our main task is to compare Sartre's *non-egology* with the Buddhist theory of selflessness *(anattā)*.

Sartre's philosophy is generally known as existentialist and Sartre himself, even after the publication of the *Critique of Dia-*

*lectical Reason*, prefers the label of existentialist to that of Marxist.[2] In *Being and Nothingness* Sartre views existentialism as a philosophy in its own right, whereas in the "Introduction" to the *Critique of Dialectical Reason* he regards existentialism as "a subordinate *ideology* which, working from within, attempts to influence the future development of Marxism."[3] Our investigation of Sartre's treatment of consciousness has been limited to his existentialism which is developed in *Being and Nothingness*. The research material is collected from all the philosophical works of Sartre except the *Critique of Dialectical Reason*.

The earliest available teaching of the Buddha is found in Pali literature which belongs to the school of the Theravādins. This school is usually accepted as *"the most orthodox school of Buddhism."*[4] Hence in the present study we use the term 'early Buddhism' to refer to Theravāda Buddhism, and in talking of 'the Buddhist,' we have the Theravādin in mind. Our discussion on the Buddhist treatment of consciousness is based on the material drawn from the Pali Canon (*Tipiṭaka*), its commentaries (*Aṭṭhakathā*) and the Pali manuals like the *Abhidhammatthasaṅgaha*.

In this comparative study we try to answer two basic questions: (1) What are the theories of self that are rejected by Sartre and the Buddhist? (2) What are the non-egological conceptions of consciousness formulated by Sartre and the Buddhist as the alternatives to the egological conceptions? To answer the first question, we consider Sartre's rejection of Husserl's doctrine of the transcendental ego in Chapter I, and the Buddhist's rejection of the Upaniṣadic theory of *ātman* in Chapter III. To answer the second question, we examine Sartre's and the Buddhist's conceptions of egoless consciousness in Chapters II and IV respectively. A thorough examination of their treatments of consciousness is undertaken in each chapter because, as is observed by Max Muller, "before we compare, we must thoroughly know what we compare."[5] In Chapter V we reflect upon what has already been discussed in the preceding chapters and, in the light of those discussions, compare and contrast Sartre's treatment of consciousness with that of the Buddhist.

## COMPARATIVE PHILOSOPHY

Since the present work is within the purview of comparative philosophy, we find it necessary to spell out our view on comparative philosophy before bringing this "Introduction" to a close.

In its loose connotation, the term "comparative philosophy" refers to a comparison of philosophical concepts from two or more different cultures with one another. But in its technical sense, the term refers to *a comparative study of Eastern and Western philosophies.*[6] Comparative philosophy, as a distinct subject, belongs to the twentieth century and is quite young. The term became popular in the West only after the publication in 1923 of P. Masson-Oursel's *La Philosophie Comparée*, an English translation of which appeared in 1926 under the title *Comparative Philosophy.*[7]

Since comparative philosophy is a relatively new subject, it is not unusual to find that its aims and methods have not been unanimously accepted by the so-called comparative philosophers. Few of them take the same approach to comparative philosophy.[8] In our opinion, the approach to comparative philosophy is primarily philosophical and secondarily historical. A historical survey of two philosophical concepts from different cultures may enable the historian of philosophy to discover that in the beginning they share the same cultural background. But the aim of comparative philosophy is not limited to this sort of historical interest. According to D.T. Suzuki, the comparative study of philosophies should bring about *"more breadth of thought and more penetrating insight into reality."*[9] This viewpoint is amplified in the following statements by N.K. Devaraja:

> *"It should result in the enrichment of his awareness of alternatives and in the sharpening of his methodological insight and critical tools. Such awareness and insights are likely to contribute to the efficiency, depth and comprehensiveness of his philosophising."*[10]

In order to realize his aim, the comparative philosopher has to pay attention not only to similarities but also to differences between the compared concepts. In comparative philosophy differences are as interesting and valuable as similarities. They are useful for self-evaluation and self-criticism. As John Taber has pointed out:

"Even when the categories of the thought of one culture do not fit those of another culture and the considerations of their respective philosophies cannot be brought mutually to bear on each other, still one often realizes thereby more distinctly what one particular philosophical tradition is *not* getting at, what is beyond its scope, which helps us to understand better what it *is* getting at and ultimately helps us to evaluate it."[11]

Thus the main task of the comparative philosopher consists in comparing and weighing philosophical concepts from different cultures, with a view to bringing about a more penetrating insight into reality. The only consideration which differentiates the task of the comparative philosopher from that of the philosopher operating within a single culture is this: that the range and variety of conceptual constructions confronted by the latter is relatively less heterogeneous and therefore, probably, more manageable than that to which the former is exposed. This is due to the fact that the comparative philosopher is dealing with philosophical concepts which are rooted in different cultures and clothed in different languages. These two factors, i.e. cultures and languages, make the task of the comparative philosopher harder.

Philosophy does not exist in a vacuum; it has a cultural background. Philosophy does not progress in isolation, without any contact with other factors in human culture. In reality, it is subject to the influence of various "extra-philosophical factors" which include economic, social and political conditions, also religion and science.[12] For example, philosophy in India is closely connected with Indian religion, whereas philosophy in the West since the Renaissance "has been influenced by science both in regard to subject-matter and also in regard to method and aims."[13] That being so, it is doubtful whether one can have any appreciative understanding of philosophical concepts considered apart from their cultural background. It is, therefore, suggested that, in order to accompiish his task, the comparative philosopher should have familiarity with the cultures out of which the candidate concepts have emerged.

## PHILOSOPHICAL TRANSLATION

Besides cultures, languages add another difficulty to the task of the comparative philosopher. The philosophical concepts to be compared are expressed in at least two different languages. Unless the comparative philosopher knows them well he has to resort to translation. In practice, this happens quite often. How many read Plato, Kant, Sartre, the Buddha and others in the original? Translation is necessary even for the comparative philosopher who masters all the languages in which the candidate concepts are originally expressed. In the process of comparison, he can accomplish his task within only *one* of the languages involved. Hence translation is indispensable to the comparative study of philosophies.

Translation has always been a difficult art, especially when the terms to be translated are philosophical terms. The conceptual frameworks of different languages are so different that one may find it hard to translate one into another exactly. There is no precise equivalent in the language of one culture for any philosophical concept which has acquired its meaning in another.[14] One always faces difficulty in translating such English terms as "experience," "value," "transcendental," into an Eastern language, and a similar difficulty in rendering *"tao," "dharma," "saṁsāra"* into English. Each of these terms has a special connotation which is untranslatable, and has to be interpreted in the context of the original text as a whole. So there is a question as to how philosophical concepts can be compared if their exact translation is not possible.

The problem of philosophical translation is a difficult, but not insoluble, methodological problem. The Chinese scholars who tried to translate Buddhist concepts into the Chinese language have faced this problem. To solve it, they employed "a method of analogy or extending idea *(Ko yi)*."[15] By this method the Chinese scholars extended the Chinese concepts to cover aspects of reality covered by the Buddhist concepts and vice versa. This method may be fruitfully employed by the comparative philosopher to solve the problem of philosophical translation. Whenever such extension of ideas is not possible or convenient, new concepts may be formed and new words coined for them or adopted from the foreign language itself. Thus we sometimes leave such Sanskrit terms as *"nirvāṇa," "mokṣa," "karma," and "brahman"* untranslated.

## THE METHODOLOGICAL ATTITUDE

We shall now bring this "Introduction" to a close with a consideration of what may be called the "methodological attitude" of the comparative philosopher. To accomplish his task, the comparative philosopher will have to keep in mind the attitude of "impartiality."[16] That is, he has to remember that each philosophical concept which comes in for comparison has a right to be considered on what merits it can show, with no prejudice either for or against it. The comparative philosopher can become impartial if he "brackets" or "suspends" his prejudice before the systematic comparison takes place.

Keeping the attitude of impartiality in mind, we set out to compare Sartre's non-egological treatment of consciousness with that of the Buddhist, with a view to bringing about a more penetrating insight into the inner structure of consciousness.

## NOTES

1 De Silva, P., *Tangles and Webs: Comparative Studies in Existentialism, Psycho-analysis and Buddhism,* Lake House Investments Ltd., Colombo, 1976, p.x.

2 "Interview with Jean-Paul Sartre," in P.A. Schilpp (ed.), *The Philosophy of Jean-Paul Sartre,* Open Court, 1981, p.22.

3 Barnes, H.E., "Introduction" to Sartre, J-P., *Search for a Method,*

translated by H.E. Barnes, Vintage Books, New York, 1968, p.viii.

4 Bapat, P.V. (ed.), *2500 Years of Buddhism,* The Publication Division, Ministry of Information and Broadcasting, Government of India, 1956, p. 101.

5 Cited in Wach, J., *The Comparative Study of Religions,* Columbia University Press, 1958, p.xi.

6 Raju, P.T., *Lectures on Comparative Philosophy,* University of Poona, 1970, p.2.

7 Translated by V.C.C. Collum, Kegan Paul, London, 1926.

8 R. Swan Liat, J.K., "Methods of Comparative Philosophy", *Philosophy East and West,* Vol. l, No. l, 1956, p. 12.

9 Suzuki, D.T., "On Philosophical Synthesis", *Philosophy East and West,* Vol. l, No. 3, 1951, p. 6.

10 Devaraja, N.K., "Philosophy and Comparative Philosophy," *Philosophy East and West,* Vol.17, No.1-4, 1967, p.57.

11 Taber, J., "Reason, Revelation and Idealism in Śaṅkara's Vedānta," *Journal of Indian Philosophy,* Vol.9, No.3, 1981, p. 2.

12 Copleston, F., *Philosophies and Cultures,* Oxford University Press, 1980, p.5.

13 Copleston, F., *A History of Philosophy,* Vol. III, Image Books, New York, 1985, p.275.

14 Burtt, E.A., "The Problem of a World Philosophy," in W.R. lnge (ed.), *Radhakrishnan,* George Allen and Unwin Ltd., 1968, p.36.

15 Fun Yu-lan, *History of Chinese Philosophy,* Vol. II, Princeton University Press, Princeton, 1953, p. 241.

16 Burtt, E.A., "Basic Problems of Method in Harmonizing Eastern and Western Philosophy," in C.A. Moore (ed.), *Essays in East-West Philosophy,* University of Hawaii, 1951, p.114.

# PART ONE

# SELFLESSNESS IN SARTRE'S EXISTENTIALISM

# I

# SARTRE'S REJECTION OF THE TRANSCENDENTAL EGO

Sartre's existentialist theory of consciousness was a result of his challenge to Husserl's egology or "science about the ego."[1] For Husserl the ego is the *subject* of consciousness. In 1936, Sartre wrote an essay entitled *The Transcendence of the Ego* (*La Transcendence de l'Ego*) in which he held that the ego is an *object* of consciousness. In 1975, Sartre says in an interview: "I maintained that point of view even in *L'Être et le Néant:* I would still maintain it today."[2] Thus Sartre's treatment of consciousness consists of two aspects: the negative and the positive. Negatively it is a rejection of Husserl's doctrine of the transcendental ego, and positively it is a formulation of Sartre's own theory of egoless consciousness. In this chapter we shall consider the negative aspect of Sartre's treatment of consciousness.

Husserl's theory of the transcendental ego was not original.

In fact, the conception of the pure ego was originally conceived by Descartes and Kant.[3] And it is the Kantian doctrine of the ego that had much more influence on Husserl. Nevertheless Husserl, particularly with respect to the pure ego, was at first more directly influenced by Natorp than by Kant, for it was through his work that Husserl became aware of the Kantian conception of the pure ego. In order to understand Natorp's view on the ego and its influence on Husserl's thought, we need to review Kant's doctrine of the transcendental ego.

According to Kant, all empirical consciousness of representations has a necessary relation to a transcendental consciousness, i.e. a consciousness of myself as original apperception.[4] In other words, consciousness of objects is accompanied by the unity of self-consciousness; that is, all empirical consciousness belongs to one and the same transcendental consciousness which is expressed in the proposition 'I think.' Hence knowledge of any object involves not only an awareness that 'S is P' but also a judgment that 'I think that S is P.' We need not be immediately aware of the idea 'I think,' but it is involved in, and presupposed by, the ideas of which we are immediately aware. Here the proposition 'I think' expresses self-consciousness.[5] It contains the form of each and every judgment of understanding and accompanies all empirical consciousness.[6] Kant writes:

> *"It must be possible for the 'I think' to accompany all my representations: for otherwise something would be represented in me which could not be thought at all, and that is equivalent to saying that the representations would be impossible or at least would be nothing to me."*[7]

Thus the 'I think' stands for a single transcendental consciousness which effects the unity of discrete acts of empirical consciousness. This unity is called "the transcendental unity of self-consciousness."[8] It is regarded as a "transcendental presupposition"[9] because it is not given as a fact of experience, but rather presupposed as the necessary condition for experience.

It functions as the unifying principle which is *"the highest principle in the whole sphere of human knowledge."*[10]

The transcendental unity of self-consciousness does not involve knowledge of a self. Knowledge is for Kant knowledge of objects given in intuition. The transcendental consciousness or self is not an intuition, but a merely intellectual representation of the spontaneity of a thinking subject.[11] Kant points out: *"I am conscious of myself, not as I appear to myself, nor as I am in myself, but only* that *I am. This representation is a thought, not an intuition... The consciousness of self is thus very far from being a knowledge of the self."*[12] The transcendental self, being a thought, is a mere logical function since the existence of the self implied by thought is only logical. *"It is only the formal condition, namely, the logical unity of every thought, in which I abstract from all objects."*[13] The self is said to be empty of all positive attributes; it is, therefore, indescribable.

> *"We can assign no other basis for this teaching than the simple, and in its completely empty, representation 'I'; and we cannot even say that this is a concept, but only that it is a bare consciousness which accompanies all concepts. Through this I or he or it (the thing) which thinks, nothing further is represented than a transcendental subject of the thoughts* = X."[14]

The transcendental self is thus for Kant not the soul, but only the subject which is indispensable for the possibility of experience. Since the self is indescribable, we can say nothing about it, neither that it is substantial, nor that it is absolute being. According to William James, the transcendental self, when we abstract all empirical elements, "is *simply nothing."*[15]

Kant maintains that the only self we know anything positive about is the empirical *me,* not the pure I. Thus Kant distinguishes between the transcendental and the empirical self. The transcendental self, as described above, stands for the transcendental consciousness by virtue of which the self neither knows *what* it is, nor does it appear to itself, but is merely aware of the fact *that* it is. Its true nature is not identical with that of my self as known or determined. The transcendental self, being the act of determining, cannot obviously be the same as that which it determines, namely, the empirical self. The transcendental self does not come under the 'category' of existence. This is because "the subject, in which the representation of time has its original ground, cannot thereby determine its own existence in time."[16] The empirical self, on the other hand, is an object among other objects and thus recognized to be a phenomenal thing appearing in the form of time. It is the self which belongs to the natural order of the world and is subject to the limitations of space and time. We yield knowledge of the empirical self by means of inner sense or inner perception and so the knowledge we receive about it is strictly empirical. "Consciousness of self according to the determinations of our state in inner perception is merely empirical, and always changing. No fixed and abiding self can present itself in the flux of inner appearances."[17]

Kant's distinction between the empirical and the transcendental self is best understood as a distinction between the contingent, discernible content or matter of our experiences and their necessary form. When he talks of the empirical self he is referring to the contingent or empirical features of experiences. When he talks of the transcendental self he is reminding us of the principle of unity of experiences. It should be noted here that the unity of experiences is impossible apart from the empirical contents of experiences, and the contents cannot be unified without the transcendental self. The self performs the form-giving activity: it is the source of all unity, for the manifold as given has no unity of its own. The transcendental unity of self-consciousness is original and not derivative; it is necessary whatever be the matter given to thought. But it is not self-sufficient; for all thinking is ultimately about a matter given to thought. Apart from the matter, the transcendental self cannot be thought. Kant writes:

> *"The principle of the necessary unity of apperception is itself, indeed, an identical, and therefore analytic, proposition; nevertheless it reveals the necessity of a synthesis of the manifold given in intuition,*

*without which the thoroughgoing identity of self-consciousness cannot be thought."*[18]

This view, as we shall see, is accepted by Sartre who says that *"consciousness is aware of itself in so far as it is consciousness of a transcendent object."*[19] That is, self-consciousness is unthinkable without consciousness of something.

## NATORP'S INTERPRETATION OF THE EGO

The Kantian doctrine of the transcendental self or ego was described again by Natorp, who belonged to the neo-Kantian philosophical movement which flourished in Germany at the time of the original publication of Husserl's Logical Investigations. In his *Introduction into Psychology according to the Critical Method,* Natorp maintains that the pure ego belongs to consciousness *"as the other point of reference besides that of which there is consciousness."*[20] According to him, the ego provides the unitary centre of relation, to which all conscious contents are referred in a wholly peculiar fashion. He, therefore, distinguishes between the contents of consciousness and the pure ego to which these contents are related. The ego cannot itself be a content of consciousness. Natorp makes it explicit that the pure ego is totally different from the contents of consciousness in that it is conscious of them whereas the latter are not conscious of the former. For this reason, Natorp does not consider the pure ego to be a phenomenological datum which can manifest itself in a phenomenological enquiry. On the contrary, he, like Kant, accepts the ego as a supposition necessarily posited, not as fact and appearance, but as the ground of all fact and appearing, *"as the ultimate ground of being with regard to the unification and, accordingly, as the possibility of unity—in a word, as the ground of the unity at large."*[21]

## HUSSERL'S DISAGREEMENT WITH NATORP

Husserl, in the first edition of the *Logical Investigations,* examines Natorp's view on the pure ego and flatly denies its existence. He says that *"I must frankly confess, however, that I am quite unable to find this ego, this primitive, necessary centre of relations."*[22] He claims that all he can find is *"the empirical ego and its empirical relations to its own experience."*[23] This empirical ego is the whole person which, if body is stripped off, would result in a "phenomenologically reduced ego." For Husserl, this ego would sufficiently account for the unity of conscious experience, being nothing but the unity of connections between experiences.[24] Hence the 'reduced ego' is at most a dependent aspect of the empirical ego.

Husserl substantiates this view by saying that in the case of a "straight-forward experience" the ego is not given as part or component of the intentional act. It is only on the basis of reflection that a mental state can come to be characterized as a state of the ego.[25] This is to say that the ego is given through reflection and cannot be given except through reflection. Husserl, furthermore, identifies this phenomenologically reduced ego with the stream of consciousness as the unity of consciousness resulting from *"psychic states interweaving with one another."*[26] *"Obviously the ego is no special entity floating above the multiplicity of experiences; rather, it is just the unity resulting from their connection with one another."*[27]

The phenomenologically reduced ego, therefore, is nothing other than the unity of consciousness, a complex of mental states. These mental states are united into complexes because of their co-existence and succession and because of the relation the states of consciousness bear to one another, but not by virtue of a special entity distinct from these mental states. In this theory there is obviously no place for the pure ego functioning as a unifying principle of discrete mental states.

> *"These contents have, as contents generally have, their own law-bound ways of coming together, of losing themselves in more*

*comprehensive unities, and, in so far as they thus become and are one, the phenomenological ego or unity of consciousness is already constituted, without need of an additional, peculiar ego-principle which supports all contents and unites them all once again.*"[28]

In the second edition of *Logical Investigations,* Husserl abandons this non-egological conception of consciousness and endorses Natorp's conception of the pure ego. In a footnote found in this second edition Husserl remarks: "I have since managed to find it (the pure ego), i.e. have learned not to be led astray from a pure grasp of the given through corrupt forms of metaphysic."[29] In another footnote Husserl points out that the empirical ego is as much a case of transcendence as physical things. If the suspension of all transcendence, through the reduction, leaves us with no residual pure ego, there can be no real and adequate self-evidence attached to the I am. *"But if there is really such an adequate self-evidence, how can one avoid assuming a pure ego?"*[30]

## THE TRANSCENDENTAL TURN

Later on Husserl, in his *Ideas,* reverses his own position maintained in *Logical Investigations.* He makes what he calls "the transcendental turn."[31] He finds it necessary to introduce the transcendental ego if he wants to characterize the phenomenological sphere. This sphere is characterized by its immanence. Husserl makes it very explicit that the following 'norm' or 'standard' has to be followed by the phenomenologist: *"To claim nothing that we cannot make essentially transparent to ourselves by reference to consciousness and on purely immanent line."*[32]

What Husserl means by the term 'immanence' can be gathered from the following statements:

*"Under acts immanently directed, or to put it more generally, under intentional experiences immanently related, we include those acts which are essentially so constituted that their intentional objects, when these exist at all, belong to the same stream of experience as*

*themselves. We have an instance of this whenever an act is related to an act (a* cogitatio *to a* cogitatio*) of the same Ego."* [33]

The point here is this: in order to make clear what immanently directed acts are, Husserl must already have the notion of "the same stream of experience." And to make the notion of "the same stream of experience" intelligible, Husserl falls back on the notion of the transcendental ego which effects this self-sameness of one stream of experience. That is, experiences belong to one and the same stream if and only if they are constituted by the same transcendental ego. The ego, therefore, is one with respect to one stream of experience.

If it is true that phenomenology depends on the notion of "immanent directedness" then it will depend on the notion of the transcendental ego. It should come as no surprise that later Husserl is finally driven to accept the following with respect to transcendental phenomenology: *"Apparently my (the philosopher's) transcendental ego is, and must be, not only its initial but its sole theme."*[34]

Thus Husserl's turn to the transcendental ego is not just an interesting but relatively unimportant 'aside'; it is a turn to the heart of consciousness in order to characterize the phenomenological sphere and the notion of immanent directedness which depends on the unity of consciousness. That is why Husserl considers consciousness to be *"the basic field of phenomenology,"*[35] and makes a complete analysis of its structure

The entire structure of consciousness, when analyzed, appears to consist of three components, namely the transcendental ego, consciousness and the intentional object. To express this triad, Husserl uses the phrase *"ego-cogito-Cogitatum."*[36] The expression 'consciousness' is used to include all experiences of the ego.[37] Husserl often uses the Cartesian term 'cogito' to refer to consciousness. *"As is known, Descartes understood this in a sense so wide as to include every case of 'I perceive, I remember, I fancy, I judge, feel, desire, will', and all experiences of the Ego."*[38] The essential nature of every cogito is to be consciousness of something:[39] that is, the cogito is 'intentionally related' to cogitatum or intentional object.

## THE TRANSCENDENTAL EGO

The transcendental ego is not the same as the cogito or consciousness: it is a unity-pole from which all acts of consciousness arise. *"Every* cogito, *every act in a specially marked sense, is characterized as act of the Ego, 'proceeding from the Ego', 'actually living' in it."*[40] Hence the ego is not an act of consciousness, nor is it an aspect of the act. While all conscious acts disappear in time, the ego is constant. It remains self-identical as acts succeed one another.

> *"In principle, at any rate, every cogito can change, can come and go, even though it may be open to doubt whether each is necessarily perishable, and not merely, as we find it, perishable in point of fact. But in contrast the pure Ego appears to be necessary in principle, and as that which remains absolutely self-identical in all real and possible change of experience, it can in no sense be reckoned as a real part or phase of the experiences themselves."*[41]

By virtue of their very structure, all conscious acts are necessarily related to the source of their origin, i.e. the ego. The ego in turn is necessarily present in and fundamentally accompanies every act. The 'ray' or 'glance' of the ego is directed via the act to the intentional object. The ego *"belongs to every experience that comes and streams past, its 'glance' goes 'through' every actual* cogito, *and towards the object. This visual ray changes with every* cogito, *shooting forth afresh with each new one as it comes, and disappearing with it. But the Ego remains self-identical."*[41a]

Thus the ego 'lives' in conscious acts in the sense that its ray goes through them towards objects. This is to say that the ego lives in every act in a special sense corresponding to the specific nature of the act in question: in perception it is a pure perceiving ego, in phantasy it is a pure phantasizing ego, in wishing it is a pure wishing ego, etc. It is, however, a ray of one and the same ego which lives in respectively varying 'modes of life'.

What is called 'living in' is a matter of describing the ways in which the rays of the ego engage in conscious acts.

> *"The attending ray gives itself as radiating from the pure Ego and as terminating in the objective, being directed towards it or deviating from it. The shaft of attention is not separate from the Ego, but itself is and remains personal."*[42]

The ego is a free being; it goes out of itself, comes back to itself, acts spontaneously, suffers, and so forth.

## KANT AND HUSSERL ON THE EGO

The transcendental ego which lives in all acts of consciousness effects the unity of these acts. The ego is the necessary ground of one stream of consciousness. A function of the ego is to give the unity to experiences. Thus Husserl establishes the ego as the principle necessary for the unity of experiences. In this respect Husserl's conception of the ego is similar to Kant's. That Husserl is in agreement with Kant is obvious from this statement:

> *"All experiences as belonging to one single stream of experiences, that, namely, which is mine, must permit of being transformed into actual* cogitationes *or of being inwardly absorbed into such; in the words of Kant, 'The "I think" must be able to accompany all my presentations.'"*[43]

However, this agreement between the two thinkers should not make us overlook their differences. The transcendental ego for Kant is a logical, formal subject of experience; it is empty apart from its empirical contents. Since the ego is not self-sufficient it cannot exist in itself. For Husserl, the ego is not a mere logical condition of experience: it is not *"an Ego conjured into being as an empty logical possibility,"* but it is an 'actual Ego' which is *"the demonstrable unity of its systematic experiences."*[44] Although it is empty apart from its conscious acts, the ego can exist in itself. *"The ego"*, writes Husserl, *"is himself existent for himself in continuous evidence; thus, in himself, he is continuously constituting himself as existing."*[45] The transcendental ego itself is not ontologically dependent upon anything else; and, therefore, the only real absolute is the transcendental ego, all else being ontologically dependent on it or relative to it.

> *"The result ... is that only transcendental subjectivity has ontologically the meaning of Absolute Being, that it only is non-relative, that is relative only to itself, whereas the real world indeed exists, but in respect to essence is relative to transcendental subjectivity, and in such a way that it can have its meaning as existing reality only as the intentional meaning-product of transcendental subjectivity."*[46]

Thus the ego for Husserl is not a *form-giving* subject but a *meaning-giving* subject. And the meaning-giving activity differentiates the Husserlian ego from the Kantian ego, which provides only a form of unity to experiences. For Husserl the ego itself is the origin or ground of experience, it constitutes the meaning of the world through its conscious acts. The ego is 'actual' because it lives in consciousness. When the ego is actually living in a conscious act, that act is said to be an 'operated act,' and the ego is the 'operative subject.' This is the most characteristic role of the ego as treated by Husserl in the *Ideas.*[47]

Another point of discrepancy between Kant and Husserl lies in the fact that whereas the former takes the ego to be a *'transcendental presupposition'*[48] the latter views it as a *'phenomenological datum.'*[49] Since the ego for Kant is "a thought, not an intuition", it cannot be contained in the data of experience. We are conscious *a priori* of the ego.[50] We cannot reflect upon it. Unlike Kant, Husserl thinks that the ego is contained in the data as a 'ray' or 'glance.'

> *"It is for Husserl the condition of the possibility of experiences all right but is yet somehow contained in the data—something which is* ipso facto *impossible in Kant's view."*[51]

Thus the ego for Husserl is available in reflection. The ego, however, is not grasped by the 'natural reflection' of everyday life; it is grasped by "transcendental-phenomenological reflection" in which "we deliver ourselves from the footing, by universal epoche, with respect to the being or non-being of the world."[52] The ego is accessible to each of us as soon as the phenomenological reduction, which is reflective by nature, is performed.

> *"By phenomenological epoche I reduce my natural human Ego and my psychic life—the realm of my psychological experience—to my transcendental-phenomenological Ego, the realm of transcendental-phenomenological self-experience."*[53]

In the *Ideas,* Husserl says that when he performs the phenomenological epoche, the empirical ego and the whole world of the natural attitude are suspended. What remains as residue is "the pure experience as act with its own proper essence." And the act is found to be related to the transcendental ego. "No disconnecting can remove the form of the *cogito* and cancel the 'pure' subject of the act."[54] Each act of consciousness "is just something 'from the Ego,' or in the reverse direction 'to the Ego': and this Ego is the pure Ego, and no reduction can get any grip on it."[55] Now it is clear that an apprehension of the ego is an outcome of the operation of the phenomenological reduction. Without the reduction, the apprehension of the ego is not possible. The reduction, therefore, turns out to be "the necessary operation which renders 'pure' consciousness accessible to us, and subsequently the whole phenomenological region."[56] If the phenomenological reduction had not been devised, the whole phenomenological region would have been unknown.[57]

## IMMANENT TRANSCENDENCE

The foregoing discussion enables us to assume that the transcendental ego is treated as a phenomenological datum in so far as it is rendered accessible to us by means of the phenomenological reduction. And the ego remains irreducible after the reduction because it is characterized by a unique type of transcendence, i.e. immanent transcendence. Husserl writes:

> *"If as residuum of the phenomenological suspension of the world and the empirical subjectivity that belongs to it there remains a pure Ego (a fundamental different one, then, for each separate stream of experience), a* quite peculiar *transcendence simultaneously presents itself—a non-constituted transcendence*—a transcendence in immanence."[58]

Hence the ego is "a transcendent in a totally different sense from the transcendent in the sense of the world."[59] To understand transcendence in this peculiar sense, we must first understand the distinction of immanence and transcendence.

Acts of consciousness can be intentionally related to other acts in the same stream of consciousness, as in the case of reflection upon past conscious acts. The totality of conscious acts making up a stream of consciousness Husserl calls "immanence."[60] When one conscious act is the intentional object of another act in the same stream, it is called "immanent object." In contrast to immanently intentive acts, there are acts which are intentive to things *beyond* the stream, beyond the immanence. Such conscious acts thus have "transcendences" as their intentional objects, e.g. real objects, ideal objects, etc. But these objects are transcendent of the immanent stream. When the ego is said to be transcendent, it is said to be in some way beyond the immanent stream. It may be useful to speak of "outward" and "inward" transcendences in order to avoid confusion. That is, the transcendent objects in general may be called *"outwardly transcendent"* while the transcendental ego may be called *"inwardly transcendent."*

The transcendental ego, therefore, is inward transcendence residing within the immanent stream of consciousness. The ego is not a part of the stream: rather it is the ground of the stream. In principle the ego can be distinguished from the stream of consciousness. "In this connection," writes Husserl, "we continue to distinguish—despite the necessary inter-relationship—the experience itself from the pure Ego of the experiencing process."[61] When it is abstracted from its conscious acts, the ego is empty of all determinations and hence indescribable. "Apart from its 'way of being related' or 'way of behaving', it is completely empty of essential components, it has no content that could be unravelled, it is in and for itself indescribable; pure ego and nothing further."[62] That is why it is so difficult to give determinations of the ego other than to say that it is permanent, identical and necessary. One affirmation alone is possible with regard to it: it is the transcendental subject of its intentional life. Husserl even goes so far as to claim that the transcendental ego cannot be "made into an object of inquiry on its own account," in other words, that it cannot be the proper theme of a study.[63] In phenomenology this is a surprising result to say the least.

## THE EGO'S PROPERTIES

However, even if the ego is indescribable, even if in some sense it is nothing, we would be wrong to think that it has nothing. The ego is empty only in abstraction. In its concreteness, the ego contains some properties; it is not contentless. In Husserl's words, "the Ego constitutes himself as identical substrate of *Ego-properties,* he constitutes himself also as a 'fixed and abiding' personal Ego."[64] By this statement Husserl means that every conscious act emanating from the ego possesses the power of sedimenting on the ego itself. Each act leaves a 'trace' on the ego, a determination which contributes to the concreteness of the ego. With every act, the ego acquires "a new abiding property." It is in this sense that the ego which has perceived a certain object is other than the ego which has perceived any other object. All position-taking likewise sediments on the ego. For example, in an act of judgment, the ego decides for the first time in favour of a being-thus. Then the act disappears. But from that moment onwards the ego is abidingly the ego who is thus and so decided, "I am of this conviction." This conviction remains abidingly the ego's property up to the time of its cancellation.

As long as the conviction is accepted by the ego, the ego finds itself "as the ego who is convinced, who, as the persisting ego, is determined by this abiding habitus or state."[65] This is true in the case of decisions of every other kind, value-decisions, volitional decisions, etc. The ego decides, the act-process vanishes, but the decision persists, sedimenting on the ego.

Thus the ego gradually emerges as a pure ego of a relatively constant style, since these sedimented determinations are stable unless new determinations explicitly come to erase them. These intentional sediments thus constitute stable properties of the ego, which Husserl expresses by the word "habitus." These are properties which the ego possesses and which contribute to giving the pure ego a personal physiognomy. The total collection of habitualities sedimented on the ego makes possible a first definition of the 'person.'[66] Husserl distinguishes sharply between a pure ego, a concrete ego constituted by the habitual sediments of its own acts, and intentional acts. The pure ego is manifested in intentional acts; this is where the ego "comes and goes." But what persists of these intentional acts contributes to the proper domain of the concrete ego or monad. In its concreteness, the ego has a history of development in the sense of being dynamic; it is no longer a static, formal subject as Kant's transcendental ego is. The concreteness of Husserl's ego contributes to giving it the status of a 'living' subject which has development in time. "To speak of the subject as temporal moreover leads forward to Heidegger rather than back to Kant ."[67]

## TRANSCENDENTAL-PHENOMENOLOGICAL IDEALISM

Husserl's doctrine of the transcendental ego has led him to regard his philosophy as a "transcendental-phenomenological idealism."[68] The idealistic trend is apparent in his view that the world is nothing other than what the ego is aware of and what appears valid in its cogitations. "The whole meaning and reality of the world rests exclusively on such cogitations."[69] Again, "the being of the pure ego and his cogitations, as a being that is prior in itself, is antecedent to the natural being of the world. ...

Natural being is a realm whose existential status is secondary: it continuously presupposes the realm of transcendental being."[70] Thus, having been an antipsychologistic 'realist' in the *Logical Investigations,* Husserl ended as an idealist in the *Ideas* and the *Cartesian Meditations.* He maintains that the *esse* of a *noema* consists exclusively in its *percipi.*[71] The world and its objects cannot be thought of except as being "constituted" by the transcendental ego's intentional acts.

> *"This world, with all its objects, I said, derives its whole sense and its existential status, which it has for me, from me myself, from me as the transcendental Ego, the Ego who comes to the fore only with the transcendental-phenomenological epoche."*[72]

The constituting function of the ego means that objects are dependent for various other characteristics upon the acts of the ego. A meaning attached to an object is a mere 'product' of the intentional acts. As such, the object can no longer be investigated in its own right. The affirmation of the ego seems to reverse the initial claim of phenomenology to return "to the things themselves" (*Zu den sachen selbst*).[73] To many disciples of Husserl, such a 'transcendental turn' in phenomenology amounts to a betrayal of what is most fruitful in the phenomenologist's emphasis upon the intentionality of consciousness. In order to reinstate the object of consciousness in its primacy, they reject Husserl's doctrine of the transcendental ego. And among the dissidents, Jean-Paul Sartre is outspoken.

## SARTRE'S REJECTION OF THE TRANSCENDENTAL EGO

Sartre's rejection of Husserl's doctrine of the transcendental ego is the main theme of his first major philosophical essay, *The Transcendence of the Ego,* the point of view of which is continued in *Being and Nothingness.* In spite of their disagreement on the ego-doctrine, there is a family relationship between Husserl's phenomenology and Sartre's existentialism. The ground of their relationship is Husserl's theory of intentionality of consciousness. Sartre's existentialism derives from a critique and modification of that Husserlian doctrine.

Husserl's theory of intentionality has been modified in Sartre's philosophy. Whereas for Husserl intentionality is one essential feature of any consciousness, for Sartre intentionality *is* consciousness. Sartre writes: "Indeed, *consciousness is defined by intentionality*. By intentionality consciousness transcends itself."[74] Consciousness is not self-enclosed; it is intentional. Consciousness aims at things beyond it; it directs itself outwards. In the article entitled "Intentionality: A Fundamental Idea of Husserl's Phenomenology," Sartre clearly says: "To be is to fly out into the world, to spring from the nothingness of the world and of consciousness in order suddenly to burst out as consciousness-in-the-world."[75] This bursting out of consciousness into the world makes it impossible that anything should be in consciousness. Thus "The object of consciousness is as a matter of principle outside consciousness (except in the case of reflective consciousness), or is transcendent."[76]

With this view of intentionality in mind, Sartre rejects Husserl's theory that the ego is the transcendental subject living in consciousness. For Sartre, there is only the empirical ego as an object outside consciousness. "The ego was a sort of *quasi-object* of consciousness and consequently, was excluded from consciousness."[77] The ego "is outside, in the world. It is a being of the world, like the ego of another."[78] Hence consciousness is without the ego: it is egoless.

In *The Transcendence of the Ego* Sartre begins his arguments with an attack on what he calls "the theory of the formal presence of the I."[79] In Sartre's view, this theory, which is held by the neo-Kantians and Husserl, affirms the ego's "formal presence at the heart of *Erlebnisse*, as an empty principle of unification."[80] It proposes that the existence of the transcendental ego is to be justified by the need that consciousness has for unity and individuality. In rejecting this theory, Sartre says that "phenomenology does not need to appeal to any such unifying and individualizing I."[81] Sartre, however, does not attack the demand that consciousness must be construed as unified and individualized, but he attacks the conviction that the transcendental ego has to be introduced to meet such a demand. He even 'concedes' to Kant that the 'I think' must be able to accompany all our representations.[82]

Sartre rightly identifies Kant's 'transcendental I' with 'transcendental consciousness' and remarks that it is "nothing but the set of conditions which are necessary for the existence of an empirical consciousness."[83] But Sartre cannot mean by this 'transcendental I' the unifying principle of consciousness. Sartre asks: "Need we then conclude that an I in fact inhabits all our states of consciousness and actually effects the supreme synthesis of our experience?"[84] He disclaims the validity of such an inference and insists that it would violate the Kantian view:

> *"Consequently, to make into a reality the transcendental I, to make it the inseparable companion of each of our 'consciousness', is to pass on fact, not on validity, and to take a point of view radically different from that of Kant."*[85]

It is precisely this, the "making into a reality the transcendental I," with which Sartre charges some neo-Kantians and Husserl. The passage in which Sartre charges Husserl with deviating from Kant is worth quoting here:

> *"If we reject all the more or less forced interpretations of the 'I think' offered by the post-Kantians, and nevertheless wish to solve the problem of the existence in fact of the I in consciousness, we meet on our path the phenomenology of Husserl.... Husserl, too, discovers the transcendental consciousness of Kant, and grasps it by the epoche. But this consciousness is no longer a set of logical conditions. It is a fact which is absolute."*[86]

## UNITY OF CONSCIOUSNESS

Thus Sartre does not agree with Husserl when the latter grants "actual existence" to the transcendental I and regards it as the absolute being. As we saw, Husserl introduces the transcendental ego in order to justify the self-sameness of the immanent stream of experience. Without the ego, the unity of consciousness cannot be accounted for. Sartre says that the transcendental ego has no place in phenomenological doctrines since there is no function which it might assume. For Husserl the function imputed to the ego is to unify conscious acts. Sartre thinks that this function is performed, not by the ego, but by consciousness itself. It is important to emphasize here that for Sartre consciousness is continual. The Bergsonian notion of an 'enduring' consciousness is not acceptable to him.[87] According to Bergson, the enduring consciousness is a flowing process, as opposed to a succession of separate events. Bergson writes: "In consciousness we find states which succeed, without being distinguished from one another ... succession without mutual externality."[88] Our conscious states are not discrete multiplicity. "There is for us nothing that is instantaneous."[89] Unlike Bergson, Sartre accepts Husserl's instantaneous conception of consciousness in *The Transcendence of the Ego.* Thus consciousness for Sartre is instantaneous or momentary.[90] Each instant of consciousness is a new existence which does not arise out of a prior instant. The rapid succession of instants constitutes one stream of experience. The instants are unified. What, then, effects the unity of discrete instants of consciousness?

Sartre, following Husserl, admits two kinds of unity of consciousness. There is, first, a unity among all those conscious acts which are directed toward the same object, for example, among all operations of adding two and two to make four. According to Sartre, this unity exists in regard to the identical object upon which every one of the acts in question bears, so that all of them must be characterized as *consciousness of this object.* This unity exists only in this respect, the acts may be separated in any way whatsoever. Hence it is not real unity. It depends upon the intentionality of consciousness; that is, conscious acts are unified by their intentional reference to self-identical, temporally continuous objects. That is why Sartre says that "it is in the object that the unity of consciousness is found."[91]

The second kind of unity is a real one; it is called the "unity within duration."[92] It is the unity of conscious acts in their duration, the unification of acts present and past, so that consciousness as a whole becomes endowed with a streamlike character. This unity is needed if "the continual flux of consciousness is to be capable of positing transcendent objects outside the flux."[93] Unity of this kind is effected neither by the intentional objects nor by any causal relation between conscious acts. Sartre writes elsewhere: "Between two consciousnesses there is no cause and effect relationship. ... One consciousness is not the cause of another."[94] This does not imply that the unity of consciousness is effected by the ego. It is significant, Sartre points out, that in accounting for the unity within duration, in *The Phenomenology of Internal Time Consciousness,* Husserl never has recourse to a synthetic power of the ego. The unity of consciousness in no way depends upon the ego.

> *"It is consciousness which unifies itself, concretely, by a play of 'transversal' intentionalities which are concrete and real retentions of past consciousness. Thus consciousness refers perpetually to itself."*[95]

## RETENTION AND PROTENTION

Sartre, therefore, maintains that consciousness unifies itself in the manner that has been described by Husserl in *The Phenomenology of Internal Time Consciousness.*[96] In this work Husserl talks of time-consciousness as a fact of experience being constituted in the flux of consciousness. Time-consciousness is unity growing out of the inseparable relation between the different phases of consciousness. For Husserl, every present moment of consciousness contains a horizon of the immediate past and a horizon of the anticipated future. This is to say that the actual present is modified by the 'retention' of what has been and the 'protention' of what is about to become a now. The retention of the immediate past is called "primary remembrance" and the retention of relatively remote events is called "secondary remembrance." These retentions are what Sartre means by "transversal intentionalities," for he says that transversal intentionalities "are concrete and real retentions of past consciousness."[97] Hence in *The Transcendence of the Ego,* consciousness is said to unify itself by the act of retention alone. But in *The Psychology of Imagination,* Sartre contends that consciousness unifies itself by acts of retention and protention. Each consciousness is said to have intentional reference to its predecessor and successor.

> *"A consciousness is through and through a synthesis, completely withdrawn into itself: it is only at the very heart of this internal synthesis that it can join itself to another preceding or succeeding consciousness by an act of retention and protention."*[98]

Since consciousness unifies itself by acts of retention and protention, the transcendental ego is not necessary for the unity of consciousness. Besides, consciousness individualizes itself. This conception of consciousness renders the unifying and individualizing role of the transcendental ego totally useless. "The transcendental I, therefore has no *raison d'être.*"[99]

So far we have shown how Sartre attempts to deny that the transcendental ego is necessary for the unity of consciousness. Sartre, however, does not offer a new solution to the problem of the unity of consciousness. To account for such unity, Sartre makes use of Husserl's own notion of temporality of consciousness. In *Ideas,* Husserl remarks that the term temporality "indicates not only something that belongs in a general way to every single experience, but a necessary form binding experiences with experiences."[100]

Thus Sartre is right in saying that Husserl can account for the unity of experience even without having recourse to the synthetic power of the transcendental ego. Nevertheless, Husserl is of the view that the unified stream of experience belongs to the transcendental ego. As Husserl says: "Every experience, as temporal being, is an experience of its pure Ego."[101] "The stream of experience is an infinite unity, and the form of the stream is one that necessarily envelops all the experience of a pure Ego."[102] Why does Husserl insist that all experiences belong to the ego?

Because his transcendental-phenomenological reduction reveals that every conscious act is necessarily related to the ego. Hence the ego can be grasped by phenomenological reflection. This means that the ego is a phenomenological datum. Sartre is aware of this point of view, for he says that the ego for Husserl is "accessible to each of us as soon as the reduction is performed."[103] Sartre then denies that the transcendental ego remains as a residue after the reduction. Unlike Husserl, Sartre thinks that what remains after the reduction is not the transcendental ego, but the transcendental sphere of consciousness purified of all egological structure.[104] To understand Sartre's position, we must first understand the distinction between pre-reflective consciousness and reflective consciousness.

## PRE-REFLECTIVE AND REFLECTIVE CONSCIOUSNESS

It is crucial that Sartre should have made a distinction between pre-reflective consciousness and reflective consciousness. The pre-reflective consciousness is intentionally related to objects "different in kind from consciousness."[105] Its object is anything but an act of consciousness in the same stream of experience. Thus the object of the pre-reflective consciousness is generally outside the immanent stream of consciousness. For example, the perceptual consciousness of a tree is directed towards a tree which is by nature external to consciousness. If we want to apprehend the perceptual consciousness of the tree, we have to produce a new consciousness called 'reflective.' Here the reflective consciousness is directed to other conscious acts in the same stream of consciousness; it is consciousness "which takes consciousness as an object."[106] According to Sartre, there is an indissoluble unity of the pre-reflective consciousness and the reflective consciousness to the point that the reflective consciousness cannot exist without the pre-reflective consciousness to be reflected upon.[107] The pre-reflective consciousness, therefore, has ontological priority over the reflective consciousness, it is considered autonomous.[108]

Having made the distinction between the pre-reflective and the reflective consciousness, Sartre continues to say that the ego does not appear in the pre-reflective consciousness. We do not find the ego through phenomenological reflection upon the pre-reflective experience. If we take into account only what is given immediately to our experience, then we have to reject the transcendental ego. To accept the ego is to allow ourselves to be led astray by "metaphysical and critical preoccupations which have nothing to do with phenomenology."[109] In order to prove that the ego does not remain as a residue after the reduction, Sartre describes his memory of reading as follows:

I have just read a story, and I recall my reading in seeking to account for my experience. There was pre-reflective consciousness of the book, of the heroes of the novel; furthermore, there was an inner awareness of consciousness of all this. This inner awareness is called "non-positional consciousness of itself", i.e. self-consciousness. *Neither consciousness of objects nor self-consciousness was in any way experienced as related to the ego.* The latter did not appear at all. As long as an act of consciousness is experienced, no ego will present itself in any mode of givenness whatever. No act bears any reference to the ego. So Sartre declares: "There was no I in the unreflected consciousness."[110] Again, "in non-reflexive thought, I never encounter the ego, my ego; I encounter that of others. Non-reflexive consciousness is absolutely rid of the ego."[111] It is, therefore, incorrect to describe consciousness of a chair as *"I have consciousness of this chair."* What we can rightly say is that *"there is consciousness of this chair."*[112]

As we have seen, Husserl takes the ego to be a phenomenological datum because it is accessible to each of us by means of phenomenological reduction. The reduction reveals that each act of consciousness bears reference to the ego: that is, consciousness is found to be necessarily related to the ego. Sartre, on the other hand, contends that the phenomenological reduction does not lead to a discovery of the ego. After the reduction, only consciousness and self-consciousness are found, and none of them is the ego or bears reference to the ego. It should be noted here that *Husserl talks of consciousness and the ego whereas Sartre talks of consciousness and self-consciousness.* As Kant has pointed out, self-consciousness is not knowledge of the self or ego. Sartre says that in self-consciousness there is no self as an entity different from consciousness. Consciousness of something and self-consciousness are not two separable activities. Consciousness is self-conscious in the sense that, in being aware of something, it is implicitly aware of itself as being conscious of that thing. From Sartre's viewpoint, Husserl seems to have mistaken self-consciousness for the ray or glance of the ego; the Kantian 'I think' is interpreted by Husserl as the transcendental ego which, he thinks, in principle is something different from consciousness.

## THE PHENOMENOLOGICAL REDUCTION

It is interesting to note that although Husserl and Sartre employ the same method, phenomenological reduction, to enquire into the nature of consciousness, the outcome of their enquiries turns out to be different. Thus it is worth asking whether their methods, in spite of bearing the same name, are really the same. Let us try to answer this question.

In *Logical Investigations* Husserl was mainly concerned with intuiting the essence which could be arrived at only through phenomenological description of the given.[113] As yet, the phenomenological reduction had not assumed any importance. Only when Husserl realized that phenomenological description cannot give us the absolutely evident so long as we remain confined to the naturalistic stand-point, did he introduce the phenomenological reduction or *epoche.* By the phenomenological reduction Husserl understands the bracketing of all presuppositions, including our belief in the existence of the world. Husserl writes:

> *"Everything transcendent that is involved must be bracketed, or be assigned the index of indifference, of epistemological nullity, an index which indicates: the* existence *of all these transcendencies,*

*whether I believe in them or not, is not here my concern; this is not the place to make judgments about them, they are entirely irrelevant."*[114]

After bracketing, what remains over is "the pure experience as act with its own proper essence."[115] And the act is found to be related to the transcendental ego.

Husserl's phenomenological reduction is not accepted by Sartre in the sense it is understood by Husserl. Though Sartre would not object to bracketing the presuppositions, he thinks that the existence of phenomena cannot be bracketed, for it is the most immediately given. Existence, for Sartre, is co-extensive with phenomena and hence is regarded as the "self-evident *irreducible*."[116] As such, the suspension of the existence of the world is not possible. Maurice Merleau-Ponty also points out that a complete bracketing is impossible, for experience is achieved through a bodily perspective and that cannot be bracketed out.[117]

Hence the bracketing of the existence of the world is not acceptable to Sartre. He accepts only the phenomenological description which is the main feature of Husserl's reduction. *Sartre wants to describe the essence of phenomena without bracketing their existence.* His intention is obvious when he speaks of the method of phenomenological psychology:

> *"Of course, the psychologist does not perform this epoche, but remains on the terrain of the natural attitude. Nevertheless there are methods available to the phenomenologist after reduction that would be of use to the psychologist. Phenomenology is a* description *of the structures of transcendental consciousness based on intuition of the essences of these structures. This description takes place, of course, on the level of* reflection.*"*[118]

What follows from these statements is that Sartre's method is phenomenological because it rests on intuitions and descriptions of essences. It is not the same as Husserl's phenomenological reduction in that it does not bracket the existence of the world. In spite of this, Sartre calls his method phenomenological reduction because it is a *'partial reduction'*[119] in the sense that presuppositions are suspended. Sartre's method is well described as *"a phenomenological description of human existence in its situation-in-the-world."*[120] It is quite similar to the phenomenological description which Husserl himself employed for rejecting the pure ego in the *Logical Investigations.* Sartre, in *The Transcendence of the Ego,* adopts this method to enquire into the same problem, and the outcome of his enquiry clearly becomes a full vindication of Husserl's non-egological conception of consciousness as maintained in the *Logical Investigations.*

## THREE CHARACTERISTICS OF CONSCIOUSNESS

So far Sartre has attacked "the theory of the formal presence of the I" by showing that the transcendental I or ego is not present in consciousness, as a principle of unification. The transcendental ego is not only unnecessary for the unity and individuality of consciousness but also counter to the phenomenological conception of consciousness. This is to say that not only is the ego useless—what is worse, it is destructive.

> *"This superfluous I would be a hindrance. If it existed it would tear consciousness from itself; it would divide consciousness; it would slide into every consciousness like an opaque blade. The transcendental I is the death of consciousness."*[121]

What Sartre means to say is that if the transcendental ego existed, three characteristics of consciousness, namely, absoluteness, transparency and spontaneity, would be destroyed. We shall return to these characteristics in the next chapter. Suffice it to say that consciousness would lose the characteristics of absoluteness, transparency and spontaneity if the transcendental ego existed as an "inhabitant" of consciousness. First of all, the ego-endowed consciousness becomes "loaded down: consciousness has not the character which rendered it the absolute existent by virtue of non-existence. It is heavy and ponderable."[122] Furthermore, since the ego for Sartre is "opaque" in the sense that it is not adequately given, if one introduces this opacity into consciousness, one thereby destroys the transparency of consciousness. "One congeals consciousness, one darkens it.... It bears within itself the germ of opaqueness."[123] Sartre also thinks that the ego lacks original spontaneity. For him, "the ego, being an object, is *passive*,"[124] hence not spontaneous. He contends that if consciousness were endowed with the ego, its spontaneity would be restricted. "Consciousness is then no longer a spontaneity."[125]

## THE SELF-LOVE THEORY

Having rejected Husserl's doctrine of the transcendental ego, Sartre now turns to attack "the theory of the material presence of the Me." By this theory Sartre means the 'self-love' theory held by some psychologists like La Rochefoucauld. According to them, the love of self and consequently the *me* are concealed within all emotions in a thousand different forms. The *me*, if it is not present to consciousness, is hidden behind consciousness and is the magnetic pole of all our actions and desires. The unconscious *me* is therefore held to be the seat of desire, dissimulated in the familiar Freudian manner.[126] It seeks to procure the object in order to satisfy its desire. "The essential structure of each of my acts would be a *reference to myself*. The 'return to me' would be constitutive of all consciousness."[127]

According to Sartre, the me does not lie concealed within consciousness as the seat of desire, rather "it is outside, in the world."[128] In other words, the *me* is not present in the pre-reflective consciousness; it appears as an object of the reflective consciousness. The 'self-love' psychologists have made a mistake because they confuse "the essential structure of reflective acts with the essential structure of the unreflective acts."[129] To explain his view, Sartre cites the following example:

I pity Peter and I go to his assistance. At that moment only one thing exists for my consciousness, i.e. Peter-having-to-be-helped. This quality of "having-to-be-helped" lies in Peter, and acts on me like a force. Peter's distress confronts me in the world as the color of an inkstand confronts me: it belongs to the intentional correlate of the personal consciousness. If I bring help to Peter that is because I perceive immediately and without reflection his need of it, not because the *me* is invoked to relieve Peter's distress. At this level, the desire to help Peter is given to consciousness as centrifugal and as impersonal; hence there is no me.[130] That I am in a state of pity for Peter appears only on reflection. Sartre writes: "The *me* must not be sought *in* the states of unreflected consciousness, nor *behind* them. The *me* appears only with the reflective act, and as noematic correlate of a reflective intention."[131] The aspect of the I which appears on reflection is passive, acted upon by Peter's distress, and is therefore to be distinguished from its other aspect which acts in the world, perceives, enquires, and so on. These aspects are what Sartre calls respectively the me and the I.

> *"The I is the ego as the unity of actions. The me is the ego as the unity of states and of qualities. The distinction that one makes between these two aspects of one and the same reality seems to us simply functional, not to say grammatical."*[132]

## THE TRANSCENDENT EGO

Sartre thus rectifies Husserl by stating that the ego is neither formally nor materially *in* consciousness. But this does not imply that Sartre might have proceeded to claim that there is no *cogito* or the *I think* anywhere. For Sartre the cogito of Descartes is the "factual necessity." The *cogito* is personal as in the *I think* there is an I who thinks. The necessity of the *I think* is asserted by Sartre: "I can always perform my recollection whatsoever in the personal mode, and at once the I appears ... Thus it seems that there is not one of my consciousness which I do not apprehend as provided with an I."[133] Thus the ego of the *cogito*, the *I think*, does in fact emerge for Sartre. But this I is not the *transcendental* ego; it is a *transcendent* ego which does not exist on the level of the pre-reflective consciousness and hence emerges as the object of the reflective consciousness. "If the I in the *I think* affirms itself as *transcendent*, this is because the I is not of the same nature as transcendental consciousness."[134]

It is interesting to note here that Sartre's view is not different from that of Husserl in the *Logical Investigations*. As mentioned earlier, Husserl rejects the Kantian pure ego while accepting the empirical ego which appears through reflection. For Husserl this ego does not appear in straightforward, i.e. pre-reflective experience. In like manner, Sartre rejects the transcendental ego found in Husserl's later works while accepting the empirical ego as being constituted by reflection. Such an ego does not appear in the pre-reflective consciousness; it does not come into existence until the pre-reflective consciousness has been made the object of reflection. As Sartre has pointed out:

> *"Non-reflective consciousness is absolutely rid of the ego, which appears only in reflective consciousness—or rather in reflected consciousness, because reflected consciousness is already a quasi-object for reflective consciousness. Behind reflected consciousness ... lies an object that we will call ego."*[135]

As such, there is never an ego as the subject but only as the object. "The ego is not the owner of consciousness; it is the object of consciousness."[136]

## PURE AND IMPURE REFLECTION

The pre-reflective consciousness is egoless; the ego appears only when this consciousness is made the object of reflection. Hence it is reflection that personalizes the impersonal consciousness. There are two kinds of reflection; one is impure reflection and the other is pure reflection.[137] The two reflections apprehend the same data, but impure reflection affirms more than it knows by adding a new element into the reflected consciousness whereas pure reflection "keeps to the given without setting claims for the future."[138] Impure reflection is constitutive in the sense that it constitutes or creates the psyche as well as psychic temporality. By psyche Sartre understands "the Ego, its states, its qualities, and its acts."[139] Pure reflection, on the other hand, is merely descriptive: it limits itself to what is really given. Pure reflection surpasses the psyche because it allows the reflected consciousness to be instantaneous rather than reified. Although Sartre admits that pure reflection is not necessarily phenomenological reflection,[140] the latter is possible on the basis of the former; pure reflection is necessary for completing the phenomenological programme. That is why Sartre sometimes talks of "the purifying reflection of phenomenological reduction."[141]

## THE CONSTITUTION OF THE EMPIRICAL EGO

Thus it is impure reflection that constitutes or creates the ego. This ego offers itself as a permanent entity, as continuing to exist beyond the reflected conscious act which is by nature instantaneous. Thus the ego is not a part of the reflected consciousness; rather it is given through the reflected consciousness. This is in conformity with the ego's being constituted by impure reflection. We must then enquire into its constitution. The ego is not, however, constituted in a direct way. The first constituted synthetic unities are states, actions and qualities. We shall survey the constitution of these psychical objects before considering that of the ego.

"My love for Peter" or "my hatred of Peter" is a state; and it appears to the reflective consciousness. Let us suppose that just now I feel a violent repugnance for Peter. What is given to my reflection is "a consciousness of violent repugnance for Peter." It is an "instantaneous consciousness of repugnance."[142] This instantaneous act of repugnance is itself not hatred, since hatred appears as being something permanent, as something which was in the past, is just now and will be in the future. This relatively permanent hatred is constituted by impure reflection upon the instantaneous acts of repugnance. "It is the transcendent unity of this infinity of consciousness."[143]

The second kind of psychical objects is *action*. Actions such as reasoning, meditating, doubting, imagining and so on are also conceived as transcendent. They share with states the property of being the unity of an infinity of consciousness. In addition to this, the action is a concrete realization; it requires time to be accomplished.

> *"It has actualizations; it has moments. To these moments corresponds concrete, active consciousness, and the reflection which is directed on the consciousness apprehends the total action in an intuition which exhibits it as the transcendent unity of the active consciousness."*[144]

The idea behind this is that an action is continuous in time, while its appearances are discrete. This transformation is due to impure reflection.

*Dispositions* or qualities represent "the ensemble of virtues, latent traits, potentialities which constitute our character and our habits."[145] They are intermediaries between states and actions. "When we have experienced hatred several times toward different persons, or tenacious resentments, or protracted angers, we unify these diverse manifestations by intending a psychic disposition for producing them."[146] The qualities such as being angry, industrious, jealous, or ambitious are conceived as potentialities which are actualized in states.

The ego is a synthetic unity of states, actions and qualities; that is, it is a transcendent unity of three transcendent unities. The ego is nothing outside the concrete totality of these psychical objects.

> *"Undoubtedly it is transcendent to all the states which it unifies, but not as an abstract whose mission is only to unify; rather, it is the infinite totality of states and of actions which is never reducible to* an *action or to* a *state."*[147]

The ego is to psychical objects what the world is to things. But it is rather rare that the world appears in the background of things. The ego, on the contrary, always appears at the horizon of psychical objects.

> *"Each state, each action is given as incapable of being separated from the ego without abstraction."*[148]

How is the constituted ego related to its states, actions and qualities? It is neither emanation, nor actualization, but creation. The ego is conceived as creating *ex nihilo* states, actions and qualities. "The ego is the creator of its states and sustains its qualities in existence by a sort of preserving spontaneity."[149] But how can the ego be spontaneous if it is an object of reflection and hence passive? Sartre's answer is simple: this spontaneity of the ego is only a *pseudo-spontaneity*.[150] Consciousness projects its own spontaneity into the constituted ego in order to confer on the ego the creative power which is necessary to it. "But this spontaneity, represented and hypostatized in an object, becomes a degraded and bastard spontaneity."[151]

## THE POSSIBILITY OF PURE REFLECTION

Thus the ego for Sartre is not the transcendental I, but the *Me*. The ego is not the origin of experience; rather it is derived from experience, that is, it is always constituted or "made-to-be." It is a product of an objectivisation of primary consciousness, a construct out of primary instantaneousness, invested with mythical permanence. The ego is an "impure growth" in a pure field of consciousness. Why impure? Because it is ego as thing, as object of reflection. From the viewpoint of pure reflection of consciousness, the ego is degraded. This is because impure reflection, which is responsible for bringing the ego into existence, is in bad faith.[152] Frightened by its own freedom, consciousness constitutes the ego in order to make the latter "its guardian and its law."[153] By what means is the false ego exposed as such? It is by pure reflection that the ego is exposed as quasi-object of consciousness. This revelation is possible only because the reflective consciousness, whose ordinary state is one of impure reflection,[154] can purify itself. Pure reflection, however, is not an ordinary state of consciousness; it "can only be obtained as the result of a modification which it effects on itself..."[155] When pure reflection is obtained, consciousness apprehends its true ontological structure; it sees itself as incomplete unity in dispersion, with no completed self-identity.[156] Sartre claims that this sort of revelation can occur to an impersonal consciousness:

> *"One might ask why the I appears on the occasion of the* cogito, *since the* cogito, *correctly performed, is an apprehension of a pure consciousness, without any constitution of states or actions. To tell the truth, the I is not necessary here, since it is never a direct unity of consciousness. One can even suppose a consciousness performing a pure reflective act which delivers consciousness to itself as a non-personal spontaneity. Only we must realize that phenomenological reduction is never perfect."*[157]

Thus a reflective apprehension of spontaneous consciousness as nonpersonal spontaneity can be accomplished by pure reflection. "This is always possible in principle, but remains very improbable or, at least, extremely rare in our human condition."[158] This difficulty arises out of the fact that most of the time consciousness puts itself in bad faith, and, consequently, its reflection often remains impure. There is a very rare chance for consciousness to escape bad faith. The issue whether anything other than bad faith is possible will be discussed later.

By means of pure reflection, Sartre himself purifies consciousness of all egological structure. He takes the ego out of consciousness and puts it into the world. Now one question arises: If the ego has been put outside consciousness, what is left of the latter? Sartre's answer is this:

> *"In a sense, it is nothing, since all physical, psycho-physical, and psychic objects, all truths, all values are outside it; since my* me *has itself ceased to be any part of it. But this nothing is all since it is* consciousness *of all these objects."*[159]

This finding in *The Transcendence of Ego* leads Sartre to propose his conception of consciousness as nothingness (*le néant*) in *Being and Nothingness*. We shall discuss Sartre's conception of consciousness in the next chapter.

## NOTES

1 Husserl, E., "Paris Lectures", in R.C. Solomon (ed.), *Phenomenology and Existentialism,* Harper & Row, 1972, p.52.
2 "An Interview with Jean-Paul Sartre", in P.A. Schilpp (ed.), *The Philosophy of Jean-Paul Sartre,* Open Court, 1981, p.10.
3 Sukale, M., *Comparative Studies in Phenomenology,* Martinus Nijhoff, 1976, p. 10.
4 Kant, I., *Critique of Pure Reason,* Translated by Norman Kemp Smith, the Macmillan Press Ltd., 1978, A 117 n.
5 CPR. A 399.
6 CPR. A 348.
7 CPR. B 131-2.
8 CPR. B 132.
9 CPR. A 107.
10 CPR. B 135.
11 CPR. B 278.
12 CPR. B 157-8.
13 CPR. A 398.
14 CPR. A 346 = B 404.
15 James, W., *The Principles of Psychology,* Vol. I, Dover Publications Inc., New York, 1950, p.365.
16 CPR. B 422.
17 CPR. A 107.
18 CPR. B 135.
19 TE. 40.
20 Quoted by Aron Gurwitsch in *Studies in Phenomenology and Psychology,* Northwestern University Press, 1966, p. 216.
21 Ibid.
22 Husserl, E., *Logical Investigations,* Vol. II, tr. by J.N. Findlay, Routledge & Kegan Paul, London, 1977, p. 549.
23 Ibid.
24 Ibid. pp. 541, 549.
25 Ibid., p. 542.
26 Ibid., p. 535.
27 Ibid., p. 541.
28 Ibid., pp. 541-2.
29 Ibid., p. 549 n. 1.
30 Ibid., p. 544 n.l.
31 Husserl, E., *Cartesian Meditations,* tr. by Dorion Cairns, Martinus Nijhoff, 1977, section(s.) 10, p. 23.
32 Husserl, E., *Ideas,* tr. by W.R. Boyce Gibson, George Allen and Unwin, London, 1969, s. 59, pp. 176-7.

33 Ibid., s. 38, p. 124.
34 *Cartesian Meditations*, s. 13, p. 30.
35 *Ideas*, s. 50, p 155.
36 *Cartesian Meditations*, s. 21, p. 50.
37 Ideas, s. 33, p. 113.
38 Ibid., s. 34, p. 115.
39 Ibid.
40 Ibid., s. 80, p. 232.
41 Ibid., s. 57, p. 172.
41a Ibid.
42 Ibid., s. 92, p. 270.
43 Ibid., s. 57, pp 172-73.
44 Ibid., s. 47, p. 148.
45 *Cartesian Meditations*, s. 31, p 66.
46 *Ideas*, p. 21.
47 Embree, L.E., "An Interpretation of the Doctrine of the Ego in Husserl's *Ideas*" F. Kersten and R. Zaner (eds.), *Phenomenology: Continuation and Criticism*, 1973, p. 28.
48 CPR. A 107.
49 *Ideas*, s. 57, p. 173.
50 CPR. A 116.
51 Chatterjee, M., "A Phenomenological Approach to the Self", in *Self, Knowledge and Freedom*, edited by J.N. Mohanty and S.P. Banerjee, World Press, 1978, p. 189.
52 *Cartesian Meditations*, s. 15, p. 34.
53 Ibid,, s. 2, p. 26.
54 *Ideas*, s. 80, p. 233.
55 Ibid.
56 Ibid., s. 33. p. 114
57 Ibid.
58 Ibid., s. 57. p 173.
59 Ibid., s. 58. p 174.
60 Husserl, E., *The Idea of Phenomenology*, translated by W.P. Alston and G. Nakhnikian, Martinus Nijhoff, 1973, p 33.
61 *Ideas*, s. 80, p. 233.
62 Ibid.
63 Ibid.
64 *Cartesian Meditations*, s. 32, p. 67.
65 Ibid.
66 Ibid.
67 Chatterjee, M., op. cit., p 189.
68 *Ideas*, p 18.
69 "Paris Lectures", p 48.
70 *Cartesian Meditations*, s. 8, p. 21.
71 Ideas, s. 98, p. 287.
72 *Cartesian Meditations*, s. 11, p. 26.
73 Thevenaz, P, *What is Phenomenology?* Quadrangle Books, Chicago, 1962, p. 41.

74 Sartre, J-P., *The Transcendence of the Ego,* tr. by F. Williams and R. Kirkpatrick, Noonday Press, New York, 1959, p. 38.
75 Sartre, J-P., "Une Idée Fondamentale de la phénoménologie de Husserl: L'intentionnalité", *Situations I,* Gallimard, 1947, p 31.
76 Sartre, J-P., *Imagination: A Psychological Critique,* tr. by F. Williams, The University of Michigan Press, 1972, p. 131.
77 "An interview with Jean-Paul Sartre", p. 10. 78. TE. 65.
78 TE. 65.
79 TE. 33.
80 TE. 31.
81 TE. 38.
82 TE. 32.
83 TE. 33; cf. CPR. A 117. n.
84 TE. 32.
85 TE. 33.
86 TE. 35.
87 Sartre, J-P., *Being and Nothingness,* tr. by Hazel E. Barnes, Pocket Books, New York, 1966, p. 194.
88 Bergson, H., *Time and Free Will,* George Allen & Unwin, 1928, p. 227.
89 Bergson, H., *Matter and Memory,* p. 56.
90 TE. 62-3.
91 TE. 38.
92 TE. 38.
93 TE. 38.
94 Sartre, J-P., *The Psychology of Imagination,* tr. by B. Frechtman, Methuen, London, 1978 p. 27.
95 TE. 39.
96 Tr. by James S. Churchill, Indiana University Press, 1966.
97 TE. 39.
98 *The Psychology of Imagination,* p. 27.
99 TE. 40.
100 *Ideas,* s. 81, p. 236.
101 Ibid.
102 Ibid., s 82 p. 238.
103 TE. 35.
104 TE 93, 96.
105 *The Psychology Of Imagination,* p. 10.
106 TE. 44.
107 TE. 44.
108 TE. 58.
109 TE. 50-51.
110 TE. 47.
111 "An Interview with Jean-Paul Sartre", p. 11.
112 TE. 53-4.
113 Bhadra, M.K., *A Critical Study of Sartre's Ontology of Consciousness,* The University of Burdwan, 1978, p. 11.
114 *The Idea of Phenomenology,* p. 31.

115 *Ideas*, s. 80, p. 233.
116 BN. 722.
117 Edie, J., "Phenomenology as a Rigorous Science", *International Philosophical Quarterly*, March 1951, p. 28.
118 Sartre, J-P., *Imagination: A Psychological Critique*, p. 128.
119 Giorgi, A., "Sartre's Systematic Psychology", P.A. Schilpp (ed.), The Philosophy of Jean-Paul Sartre, p. 195
120 Williams, F. and Kirkpatrick, R., "Translator's Introduction" to *The Transcendence of the Ego*, p. 25.
121 TE. 40.
122 TE. 42.
123 TE. 41-2.
124 TE. 79.
125 TE. 41.
126 Caws, P., *Sartre*, Routledge & Kegan Paul, 1979, p. 56.
127 TE. 54.
128 TE. 31.
129 TE. 55.
130 TE. 56.
131 TE. 59-60.
132 TE. 60.
133 TE. 43-4
134 TE. 51.
135 "An Interview with Jean-Paul Sartre", p. 11.
136 TE. 69.
137 TE. 64: BN. 223.
138 TE. 64.
139 BN. 126.
140 TE. 64.
141 Sartre, J-P., *Sketch for a Theory of the Emotions*, tr. by Philip Mairet, Methuen & Co. Ltd., 1977, p. 91.
142 TE. 62.
143 TE. 63.
144 TE. 69.
145 BN. 226-7.
146 TE. 70.
147 TE. 74.
148 TE. 75.
149 TE. 78.
150 TE. 79.
151 TE. 81.
152 BN. 225.
153 TE. 101.
154 BN. 233-4.
155 BN. 224.
156 Kenevan, P.B., "Self-consciousness and the Ego in the Philosophy of Sartre", P A. Schilpp (ed.), *The Philosophy of Jean-Paul Sartre*, pp.202-3.

157 TE. 91.
158 TE. 92.
159 TE. 93.

# II

# THE SARTREAN CONCEPTION OF CONSCIOUSNESS

Sartre's main interest in rejecting Husserl's doctrine of the transcendental ego is to empty consciousness of all con tents. Purified of all egological structure, the pure field of consciousness recovers its primary transparency. The self-transparency of consciousness excludes the possibility that anything is in consciousness. Hence the radical consequence of Sartre's rejection of the transcendental ego is that *consciousness has no contents;* all content is on the side of the object. Sartre points out: "There is not a content of consciousness; there is—what is, in my opinion, Husserl's mistake—no subject behind consciousness, that is, something like a transcendence in immanence."[1]

Sartre defines consciousness by intentionality.[2] All consciousness is *consciousness of something;* consciousness transcends itself towards the object. Neither the object nor the image has the status of being a content of consciousness; they are outside it. All so-called 'images,' 'representations,' 'ideas,' 'phenomena,' 'sense-data,' etc., are objects *for* consciousness, not contents *in* consciousness. Sartre, like William James, insists that representational theories of knowledge violate our sense of life. When we imagine a tree, it is a tree we are imagining, not our image of a tree. Consciousness is present to objects. "There are not, and never could be, images in consciousness. Rather, image is a certain type of consciousness. An image is an act, not something. An image is a *consciousness of* something."[3]

Emptied of all contents, consciousness is characterized by spontaneity, absoluteness and transparency.[4] What are these characteristics?

## SPONTANEITY

Sartre describes consciousness as an impersonal spontaneity, a sheer activity transcending towards objects.[5] What he means by spontaneity is elucidated in these statements:

> *"That exists spontaneously which determines its own existence. In other words, to exist spontaneously is to exist for oneself and through oneself* (exister pour soi et par soi*). One reality alone deserves to be called 'spontaneous': Consciousness."*[6]

This is to say that consciousness is spontaneous because it determines its existence, without our being able to conceive anything *before* it. It is generated neither by an ego nor by any other consciousness in the same stream of experience. "One consciousness is not the cause of another."[7] "Thus each instant of our conscious life reveals to us a creation *ex nihilo.* Not a new arrangement, but a new existence."[8] Nothing (*rien*) is the cause of consciousness; it is consciousness which is the cause of its own way of being.[9] In this context, Sartre seems to use the term spontaneity in the sense of "*uncaused* origination" as opposed to "*dependent* origination." Being spontaneous or self-caused, consciousness is said to be free, for it is not subject to any causal laws. "Consciousness is frightened by its own spontaneity because it senses this spontaneity as beyond freedom."[10]

## ABSOLUTENESS

Furthermore, consciousness for Sartre is "a non-substantial absolute."[11] Sartre uses the term 'absolute' in the sense of "non-relative." He, following Husserl, makes the distinction between relative and absolute existents. Something is a relative existent when it is an object for something. The world, for example, is a relative existent because it is the object for consciousness: consciousness, on the contrary, is not relative because it is not for anything; it is a being-for-itself (*l'être-pour-soi*). Consciousness is "*a revealing intuition of something.*"[12] It is not revealed by anything other than itself. Consciousness is self-luminous or self-transparent. According to Sartre, consciousness, which is absolute, is non-substantial, because its "*existence precedes essence.*"[13] Criticizing Descartes' substantialism, Sartre says that Descartes goes wrong because he fails to see that if the absolute is defined by primacy of existence over essence, it cannot be regarded as a substance.

> *"Consciousness has nothing substantial, it is pure 'appearance' in the sense that it exists only to the degree to which it appears. But it is precisely because consciousness is pure appearance, because it is* total emptiness *(since the entire world is outside it)—it is because of this identity of appearance and existence within it that it can be considered as the absolute."*[14]

## SELF-CONSCIOUSNESS

Since its existence is identical with its appearance, consciousness exists only to the extent that it appears to itself in the mode of self-transparency or self-consciousness. In this respect, self-consciousness is regarded as the "mode of existence" of consciousness;[15] that is, "the type of existence of consciousness is to be consciousness of itself."[16] From this it follows that *self-con-*

*sciousness is the necessary condition of the existence of consciousness.* Thus self-consciousness is taken to be an essential characteristic which enables us to differentiate consciousness from a non-conscious being. As Sartre says, "to be other than being is to be self-conscious."[17]

By self-consciousness Sartre understands an immediate, non-cognitive relation of consciousness to itself.[18] In the case of self-consciousness, consciousness does not posit itself as an object; the subject-object duality does not arise here. The non-positional consciousness arrives at itself without recourse to discursive thought. Self consciousness should not be confused with the reflective consciousness which takes the reflected consciousness as its object. All consciousness is non-positional consciousness of itself in the very process of being conscious of something. That is, it is consciousness of itself as consciousness of something, or is aware of being aware. In this sense, self-consciousness and consciousness of something are mutually dependent. Apart from consciousness of something, self-consciousness is impossible. "Consciousness is aware of itself in so far as it is consciousness of a transcendent object."[19] This, however, does not imply that consciousness of something contains self-consciousness as its quality. This is because consciousness is not a thing which we may qualify with "self-conscious" as we might qualify a flower with "red." Consciousness of something and self-consciousness constitute "an indivisible, indissoluble being—definitely not a substance supporting its qualities like particles of being, but a being which is its existence through and through."[20]

According to Sartre, self-consciousness is the necessary and sufficient condition for a knowing consciousness to be knowledge of its object.[21] Alain's statement "to know is to know that one knows" is interpreted by Sartre in these words: "To know is to be conscious of knowing."[22] One may agree with Sartre that self-consciousness is the sufficient condition because to be conscious that one knows that "S is P" is to know that "S is P." But one is doubtful whether it is the necessary condition. Some philosophers deny that self-consciousness is the necessary condition of knowledge. Spinoza and the British philosopher Prichard do so, and the Scandinavian thinker, Jaakko Hintikka, believes something quite close to this.[23] Sartre, however, has offered an argument in support of his claim that self-consciousness is the necessary condition. He says:

> *"If my consciousness were not consciousness of being consciousness of the table, it would then be consciousness of that table without consciousness of being so. In other words, it would be a consciousness ignorant of itself, an unconscious—which is absurd."*[24]

There is an obvious flaw in this argument, which consists in the move from "consciousness ignorant of itself" to "unconscious." The more proper conclusion would rather be "unself-conscious". Granted that by "unconscious" Sartre means "unself-conscious," we still fail to understand why the concept of "unself-conscious consciousness" is absurd in so far as we define consciousness by intentionality. I might be conscious of this table without being conscious of being so, and there is nothing absurd about this; consciousness does not lose intentionality, which is its defining characteristic. Sartre views it as being absurd because he takes consciousness to be necessarily self-conscious. And self-consciousness enables Sartre to avoid an infinite regress. Sartre thinks that if a particular consciousness were not self-consciousness, it would be known only by the second consciousness; and the second in turn by the third, etc. The series would go on to infinity. "If we wish to avoid an infinite regress, there must be an immediate, noncognitive relation of the self to itself."[25] There is merit in Sartre's argument. Sartre can claim its validity because he gains support from phenomenological reflection. Sartre says that, in reflecting upon his experience of reading, he discovers "consciousness of the object and non-positional consciousness of itself."[26]

## TRANSPHENOMENAL BEING

Now we are in a position to say that consciousness for Sartre has two defining characteristics: intentionality and self-transparency. *Consciousness is consciousness of something*[27] *and consciousness of something is self-conscious.*[28] Self-consciousness presupposes consciousness of something for the reason that consciousness is aware of itself only when it is consciousness of something. And consciousness of something, in turn, presupposes the being of the object. By "consciousness of something" Sartre means "a revealing intuition of something i.e. of a transcendent being."[29] And the revealing intuition implies something revealed, something other than consciousness itself. "A consciousness which would be consciousness of nothing would be absolute nothing."[30] But consciousness is not an absolute nothing, for it is consciousness of something. And in so far as it is consciousness of something, this something must "have a real being—that is, a being not relative to consciousness."[31] Consciousness, therefore, implies "a non-conscious and transphenomenal being."[32]

Consequently, the being of the object is discovered without exception in every act of consciousness. Consciousness is never alone; it is never isolated from the being of the object. This means that the being of the object is the "constitutive structure" of consciousness; that is, that consciousness is born supported by the being of the object. The demand of consciousness for its object proves that there is the being of the object outside consciousness. This kind of proof is called "ontological proof."[33] Sartre thinks that the being of the object is independent of consciousness; it is "transphenomenal being" because it transcends its phenomenal condition.

> *"The being of the phenomenon, although coextensive with the phenomenon, cannot be subject to the phenomenal condition which is to exist only in so far as it reveals itself—and that consequently it surpasses the knowledge which we have of it and provides the basis for such knowledge."*[34]

It should be noted here that Husserl takes the being of the known object to be wholly dependent on the acts of the knowing subject, i.e., the transcendental ego. According to him, the *esse* of a *noema* consists exclusively in its *percipi.*[35] From Sartre's viewpoint, Husserl has reduced the being of the object to a series of meanings.[36] In contrast with Husserl's position, Sartre maintains that "the *esse* of the phenomenon cannot be its *percipi.*"[37] By asserting that the being of the object is not subject to the phenomenal condition, Sartre has proposed an approach not just different from but diametrically opposed to Husserl's. Instead of reducing being to a series of meanings, Sartre explains knowledge and meanings in terms of being, insisting that being is "the self-evident irreducible" and therefore any attempt at reducing it to something else, and thus trying to go beyond it, is impossible.[38]

## TWO TYPES OF BEING

Sartre, therefore, makes the distinction between consciousness and its object. He insists that these are two different types of being. "That there are two types of existence, as thing-in-the-world and as consciousness, is an ontological law."[39] The being of the object is called *being-in-itself* (*l'être-en-soi*), and the being of consciousness is called *being-for-itself* (*l'être-pour-soi*).[40] Since the being of the object is revealed through the phenomenological description of consciousness, Sartre's ontology is called "phenomenological ontology."[41]

*Being-in-itself* is the non-conscious being of the object of consciousness.[42] It is pure existence as such, existentia. It cannot be a thing or an ensemble of things. Neither can it be hidden behind things in the manner of the noumenon. It is the being of phenomena; that is, the pure "*that it is*" of things. This is Sartre's reappropriation of Heidegger's assertion that "Being is the *transcendens* pure and simple."[43]

The in-itself is plenitude or fullness characterized by impermeability and infinite density. It is so full of itself that it does not admit any change or becoming. "Transition, becoming, anything which permits us to say that being is not yet what it will be and that it is already what it is not—all that is forbidden on principle."[44] The in-itself is also 'uncreated,' 'not subject to temporality,' and 'undifferentiated.' It is neither possible nor necessary, but rather 'contingent.' It is wholly independent or *Selbständig*. It is thus absolutely non-referential. Lacking differentiating predicates, it can only be said to be. "Being is. Being is in-itself. Being is what it is."[45]

*Being-for-itself* is the being of consciousness which is a 'revealing intuition' of the being-in-itself. For Sartre, being-for-itself (*l'être-pour soi*), consciousness (*la conscience*) and human reality (*la réalité humane*)—all mean the same and he uses them indiscriminately. The for-itself is defined as "*being what it is not, and not being what it is.*"[46] It is a negation of the in-itself which is "what it is." If the in-itself is a fullness, then the for-itself is a lack, "total emptiness" (*un vide total*).[47] What the for-itself lacks is the being-in-itself.[48] The for-itself is thus the absence of being; "it is a hole in being at the heart of being,"[49] and because of this hole a tremendous upheaval happens to the in-itself, and this upheaval is the appearance of the world.[50] Due to the presence of the for-itself to the in-itself, the world is constituted, not in the sense of idealistically creating, but in the sense of organizing or manifesting. "Worldliness, spatiality, quantity, instrumentality, temporality—all come into being because I am the negation of being."[51] Without the for-itself there would exist no world but merely "the undifferentiated totality of being."[52] Moreover, the for-itself is not a person; that is, it is not "the totality of the human being" but rather "the instantaneous nucleus of this being."[53]

## NOTHINGNESS

Thus the for-itself or consciousness is the negation of being; it introduces a fissure into the being-in-itself. This fissure takes place whenever consciousness directs itself towards the object. This is to say that when consciousness is conscious of something, it is implicitly conscious of itself as *not being* that thing. In the case of a perceptual consciousness of a chair, for instance, there is the apprehension of the chair as the in-itself which consciousness is not. By self-consciousness, consciousness is aware of itself as not-being-the-chair. "Its not-being-the-chair is ... in the form of the consciousness (of) not-being."[54] Hence consciousness is nothingness in the sense of not being the in-itself, and it is aware of its own nothingness by means of self-consciousness. "Consciousness is a being, the nature of which is to be conscious of nothingness of its being."[55] Here we find the close connection between two Sartrean notions: *nothingness* and *self-consciousness*. We may assume that consciousness for Sartre is nothingness because it is necessarily self-conscious. Unless it were self-conscious, consciousness would not be able to tear itself away from its object, it would not be aware of itself as not being the object. Consciousness which has lapsed into the past is not self-conscious. As a result, it is no longer nothingness; it becomes a being-in-itself.[56]

Furthermore consciousness is said to be nothingness for the reason that all being is on the side of its objects. Consciousness is a total emptiness, for the entire world is outside it.[57] This, however, should not mislead us into assuming that consciousness is an absolute nothingness (*nihilum absolutum*), i.e. the absence of all being. Consciousness is not the nihilation of a great complete whole such as the Parmenidian Being. Rather, it is the nihilation of the individual in-itself. Sartre writes:

> *"It is the nihilation of an individual and particular in-itself and not of a being in general. The for-itself is not nothingness in general but a particular privation; it constitutes itself as the privation of this being."*[58]

Consciousness, as the nihilation of a particular being, has only "a borrowed existence."[59] "For consciousness there is no being except for this precise obligation to be a revealing intuition of something."[60] Without the in-itself to be revealed, consciousness cannot be self-conscious and thereby ceases to exist as "pure appearance." From this it follows that the in-itself is ontologically prior to consciousness and establishes the ground for it. Consciousness without the in-itself is a kind of abstraction; it could not exist any more than a color could exist without form.[61] This does not imply that consciousness and the in-itself are mutually dependent. The in-itself has no need of consciousness in order to be. "The phenomenon of the in-itself is an abstraction without consciousness but its being is not an abstraction."[62]

It is important to emphasize here that Sartre, when describing consciousness as nothingness, does not think that nothingness is a mere logical concept formulated through speculative reasoning. According to Sartre, nothingness, if it is a concept at all, is an experiential concept for it is derived from our experience. It is not a product of a conceptual negation; on the contrary, all the logical or propositional negations are conditioned and supported by this primordial nothingness. To demonstrate this, Sartre examines two notions: interrogation and negative judgment.

According to Sartre, it is in tracing out the questioning situation that nothingness is discovered. Every question presupposes a dyad of beings, viz. the being who questions and the being who is questioned. If I ask, for instance, "is there any conduct which can reveal to me the relation of man with the world?", I indicate my ignorance. Now ignorance or absence of knowledge is a non-being. The reply to my question can be either negative or positive. If it is in the negative, new non-being is implied. If the answer is in the affirmative, it involves a third non-being—"the non-being of limitation," for it is in the form of "it is thus and not otherwise." Hence every question addressed to being involves the possibility of this triple non-being. "The permanent possibility of non-being, outside us and within, conditions our questions about being."[63]

Sartre is aware of the objection raised by his critics that nothingness is not an experiential concept but rather a concept derived from judgments. They say that a negation arises when our expectations end in failure. For example, I believe that I have fifteen hundred francs in my pockets, and after a search I find only thirteen hundred. This does not mean that I discover the non-being of fifteen hundred francs but simply that I have counted thirteen hundred francs. "Negation proper (we are told) is unthinkable; it could appear only on the level of an act of judgment by which I should establish a comparison between the result anticipated and the result obtained."[64] Thus nothingness seems to be a result of concrete psychic operations; it is a pure subjectivity. In this sense, nothingness cannot have the "slightest trace of reality."

Sartre does not accept the view of his critics. He states that non-being does not come to things by a negative judgment; rather, it is a negative judgment which is conditioned and supported by a prejudicative comprehension of a non-being. In the example cited above, it is a comprehension of the non-being of two hundred francs that serves as foundation for making the negative judgment. Sartre writes: "The necessary condition for our saying 'not' is that non-being be a perpetual presence in us and outside, that nothingness haunts being."[65] Sartre denies that the negative judgment arises when our expectations end in failure. He, however, concedes that expectations have something to do with the negative judgment; they lead us to discover non-being. "It is evident," says Sartre, "that non-being always appears within the limits of a human expectation."[66] To substantiate his view, Sartre cites the following example:

I have an appointment with my friend Pierre at a certain cafe at four o'clock. Suppose I arrive fifteen minutes late and find that Pierre, who is always punctual, is not there. I then make a negative judgment that "Pierre is not here." The cafe where I expect to meet him is full of being. The patrons, the tables, the mirrors, the light and everything in the cafe constitute a ground against which Pierre is about to appear. This organization of the cafe as the ground for Pierre's appearance is "an original nihilation." Each thing in the cafe first appears to me as a distinct object and then falls back into the ground by my nihilating activity. The ground is the necessary condition for the appearance of the principal figure, which is here the person of Pierre. Since Pierre is absent, what appears on the ground is not his presence but his absence. "It is Pierre rising himself as nothingness on the ground of the nihilation of the cafe."[67] My intuition of Pierre's absence leads me to make the negative judgment that he is not here. And it is my expectation for Pierre's presence that leads me to discover his absence. "I myself expected to see Pierre, and my expectation has caused the absence of Pierre to happen as a real event concerning this cafe. It is an objective fact at present that I have *discovered* this absence."[68]

"This example," Sartre concludes, "is sufficient to show that non-being does not come to things by a negative judgment; it is the negative judgment, on the contrary, which is conditioned and supported by non-being."[69] Sartre asserts that nothingness is not a subjective concept resulting from man's psychic operations. Nothingness for Sartre is an objective reality; that is, the reality of nothingness is not dependent upon the acts of consciousness. According to Sartre, "there is a transphenomenality of non-being as of being."[70] He contends that nothingness can be given to our intuition. "In order for negation to exist in the world and in order that we may consequently raise questions concerning Being, it is necessary that in some way *Nothingness be given*."[71] Sartre, however, does not specify how nothingness can be given to our intuition. Just as Husserl has difficulty in showing how the transcendental ego is given to our phenomenological reflection, so also Sartre has difficulty in specifying how nothingness is given to intuition. The main problem is: If consciousness is consciousness of *something*, how can it be consciousness of *nothing*?

Sartre goes on to say that the intuitive apprehension of nothingness is necessary not only for interrogation and negative judgment but also for the manifestation of *négatités*. As Sartre himself says: "Nothingness must be given at the heart of Being, in order for us to be able to apprehend that particular type of realities which we called négatités."[72] The term 'négatités' is coined by Sartre to name experiences of realities such as destruction, change, otherness and so forth, which in their inner structure are "inhabited by negation."[73] In négatités a thing is given along with a non-being. Destruction, for example, involves non-existence of a thing which once existed. Non-being has been introduced into the thing. From where does non-being come to the thing? The thing cannot generate non-being because it is a being-in-itself, a what-it-is. "There is not the slightest emptiness in being, not the tiniest crack through which nothingness might slip in."[74] This means that nothingness cannot stem from the in-itself. Neither can nothingness generate itself. In Sartre's view, nothingness does not nihilate itself; nothingness is nihilated.

> *"It follows therefore that there must exist a Being (this cannot be the In-itself) of which the property is to nihilate Nothingness, to support it in its being, to sustain it perpetually in its very existence, a being by which nothingness comes to things."*[75]

According to Sartre, the being which introduces nothingness into things is human reality. "Man is the being through whom nothingness comes to the world."[76] Since the being by which nothingness comes to the world must be its own nothingness,[77] human reality therefore is its own nothingness.[78] This amounts to saying that consciousness is nothingness, for the term 'human reality' is used as a synonym for consciousness.

Sartre's description of the appearance of nothingness in the world can be summarized in the following statement: Since the in-itself is so full of itself that it does not admit any negative element, nothingness must be brought to things by the being which is not the in-itself; and that being is consciousness. Holding this view, Sartre has to face some difficulties. If it is true that consciousness introduces nothingness into things, then the reality of nothingness seems to be dependent upon the nihilating activity of consciousness. If this is the case, how can one say that nothingness is an objective reality? And nothingness, the reality of which depends on the acts of consciousness, cannot be transphenomenal as Sartre believes. Furthermore, it is questionable whether one can rightly speak about the "phenomenon" of non-being. How can non-being appear to our intuition? Sartre himself maintains that being is coextensive with phenomenon. As such, there can be only phenomenon of being, not phenomenon of non-being. If Sartre allows that there is phenomenon of non-being, then he has to admit, as against his own position, that there is phenomenon which is not coextensive with being. Since Sartre can never admit this implication, he has to deny that there is phenomenon of non-being. As a result, he is not in a position to claim, as he actually did, that "there is a transphenomenality of non-being as of being."[79]

## TEMPORALITY

The in-itself, as is mentioned earlier, is a full positivity that cannot admit any change or becoming. This means that the in-itself is not subject to temporality. Sartre writes: "The in-itself cannot be present any more than it can be past."[80] Now one question arises: If the in-itself is not temporal, from where does temporality come to things? To this question, Sartre's answer would be that it is consciousness which introduces temporality into things. This is because "consciousness is temporal,"[81] that is, temporality is the infra-structure or mode of being of consciousness.[82] In short, consciousness temporalizes itself.

According to Sartre, there are two temporalities: original temporality which is the infra-structure of consciousness and psychic temporality which is constituted by impure reflection.[83] Impure reflection, as has been shown in the preceding chapter, constitutes the psychic facts, viz. the ego, its states, its acts and its qualities. Psychic temporality is constituted through the succession of these psychic facts.

> *"Indeed it is their reality which is the object of* psychology. *Practically it is on the level of psychic fact that concrete relation between men are established—claims, jealousies, grudges, suggestions, struggles, rules, etc."*[84]

For Sartre, it is not conceivable that the pre-reflective consciousness, which temporalizes itself, should be itself these states, these acts and these qualities. Since these psychic facts are constituted by impure reflection, they cannot appear in the pre-reflective consciousness. Thus psychic temporality, which is the successive order of psychic facts, disappears completely if consciousness remains on the pre-reflective level or if impure reflection purifies itself. In the pre-reflective experience there is only original temporality. The pre-reflective consciousness is aware of original temporality, not in the form of reflection, but in the form of non-thetic self-consciousness.

Original temporality, for Sartre, is an 'organized structure'. The three dimensions of time, past, present and future, are not considered as an infinite series of 'nows'—but rather as "the structured moments of an original synthesis."[85] The pre-reflective consciousness, being temporal, is an 'ekstatic unity' which simultaneously exists in the three dimensions of past, present and future. Now we shall consider how the three dimensions are related to one another in such a way that their unity is formed.

## 1. THE PAST

The first dimension is the past. What is the being of the past? The answer given by some thinkers is that since the past is no longer, it has no being. This view is not acceptable to Sartre because it fails to account for the passivity of memory in which a remembering consciousness transcends the present in order to aim at an event in the past. On the other hand, some thinkers like Bergson and Husserl maintain that the past has a kind of existence. For them, being past for an event simply means being retired, losing its efficacy without losing its being. According to Sartre, this view fails to explain how the past can be related to the present. Since the past has been conferred the existence of the in-itself, it is impossible to unite it to the present. This is because of the fact that the in-itself "is isolated in its being and that it does not enter into any connection with what is not itself."[86] All bridges between the past and the present have been cut down.

According to Sartre, whether the past is or is no longer is

hardly of any importance in so far as it does not enable us to reconnect it to the present. The problem of relation arises for those philosophers who consider temporality as primarily separated instants to which they grant *a priori* being-in-itself. "This problem has for a long time been disguised by a conception of the human being as an in-itself."[87] As a result, it is not possible to establish between instants the "slightest connection of succession." Hume, for example, finds in his mind a succession of impressions each one of which is a "distinct existence." He fails to understand how these impressions are related to one another. Sartre, therefore, writes: "Any connection with an antecedent or consequent, no matter how constant it may be, remains unintelligible."[88]

To avoid such difficulty Sartre proposes that instead of considering temporality as a separation, one should approach it as a totality.[89] In doing so, one will see that the past is first of all *my* past. It is not nothing, neither is it the present, but it is bound to a certain present and to a certain future, to both of which it belongs. The past has ontological relation with the present. "It is originally the past of the present."[90] The past of a man is never cut off from his total being. Suppose we say that Paul was a student in 1940. Who was the student then? It is Paul, living at the present time, who was the student. This is to say that Paul has a past. The same is true for everyone. But one does not have a past as one has a car. In the case of having a car, the relation between the possessor and his car is an *external* relation; he can dissociate himself from it. But in the case of having a past, I cannot dissociate myself. I am related to my past in the form of an *internal* relation. I am my past in the form of "I am me."[91]

Thus the past consciousness is not separated from the present consciousness.

> *"What separates prior from subsequent is exactly nothing* (rien). *This nothing is absolutely impassable, just because it is nothing... The prior consciousness is always* there *(though with the modification of 'pastness'). It constantly maintains a relation of interpretation with the present consciousness, but on the basis of this existential relation*

*it is put out of the game, out of the circuit, between parentheses....*"[92]

This means that "the prior consciousness" is not a discrete unit but is continuously surpassed. The past is continuously added to, without a break.

Consciousness which has lapsed into the past is no longer self-consciousness; "its being is no longer for itself since it no longer exists as reflection-reflecting."[93] In this sense, the past consciousness becomes an in-itself. Thus the past is a solidification of the for-itself from which all possibility is excluded. Consciousness falling into the past becomes a being-in-the-midst-of-the-world.[94] The past is described as a for-itself inundated by the in-itself. "Like the mermaid whose human body is completed in the tail of a fish, the extra-mundane for itself is completed behind itself as a thing in the world."[95]

The present consciousness is its past, not in the mode of identity, but rather in the mode of "an internal bond of non-being." "It is not what it is."[96] This means that consciousness cannot dissociate itself from its past; it has to be it. But the present consciousness is a for-itself, it can never be identical with the past consciousness which has already become an in-itself. "In so far as it is for-itself, it is never what it is. What it is is behind it as the perpetual surpassed."[97] The past, therefore, haunts the present consciousness or the for-itself as its original contingency. This contingency Sartre calls facticity. For Sartre, the expressions "past" and "facticity" indicate one and the same thing. "It is precisely this surpassed facticity which we call the past. The past then is a necessary structure of the for-itself."[98] The past is regarded as the essence of the present consciousness. That is why Sartre says that "My essence is in the past."[99] The present consciousness exists as a "pure appearance." This present existence of consciousness precedes its essence. Thus in consciousness, "existence precedes essence."[100]

## 2. THE PRESENT

In contrast to the past consciousness which has become an in-itself, the present consciousness is characterized as the for-itself. The meaning of the present is presence to the being-in-itself. Sartre defines the present consciousness or for-itself as "presence to being."[101] Consciousness is presence to something in so far as it is a witness of itself as not being that thing. That is, when consciousness is conscious of an object, it is implicitly aware of itself as not being that object.

> *"It is consciousness of —— as the internal negation of ——. The structure at the basis of intentionality and of selfness is the* negation, *which is the internal relation of the for-itself to the thing.... It is in the mode of the for-itself; that is, as a separate existence inasmuch as* it reveals itself as not being being."[102]

The present, therefore, is an escape from being which is "there." It is a perpetual flight in the face of being. Hence the present is defined as non-being. As Sartre writes: "Thus we have precisely defined the fundamental meaning of the Present: the Present *is not*."[103] The present can never be grasped in the form of an instant, for the instant is the moment when the present is. But the present never is; it has no being which coincides with itself. The present consciousness "is not" but is rather a relation between the past and the future across the chasm that is itself. It is a "chasm" that divides non-temporal plenitude into a before and an after, a "detotalized totality."[104] The present consciousness is the reference point relative to which there is a past and a future "down there, in the distance." It has being outside of it, before and behind. "Before itself, behind itself; never itself"[105] is the description of the present. Before itself, it has to be its future; and behind itself, it has to be its past. "At present it is not what it is (past) and it is what it is not (future)."[106]

### 3. THE FUTURE

The present is a flight out of the past into the future. What, then, is the future? According to Sartre, "the future is what I have to be in so far as I cannot be it."[107] At present the for-itself is a lack.

This lack or nothingness is the inner structure of the for-itself. Consciousness does not exist first in order afterwards to lack this or that; it exists first as lack and in immediate connection with what it lacks.[108] What the for-itself lacks is the self-as-being-in-itself.[109] It projects itself into the future in order to unite itself with the lacking; that is, with that which, if added to its present, would make it be what it is. Thus the for-itself is by nature the transcendence or "the project of self beyond."[110] It is its own surpassing towards its ideal which, if realized, would transform the for-itself into the in-itself-for-itself. This ideal, however, is unrealizable. The future does not allow itself to be rejoined; it slides into the past as a by-gone future, and the for-itself once again is a lack of a new future.

The past is that in which all possibility is ruled out, whereas the future "is simply my possibility of presence to being beyond being."[111] Sartre has defined possibility in these words: "What is given as the peculiar lack of each for-itself and what is strictly defined as lacking to precisely this for-itself and no other is the possibility of the for-itself."[112] The future is regarded as a project of possibility for the reason that it presents us with a fragility of that which could be and could also not be. And it is due to the freedom of the for-itself that the future is the possibility rather than determination. "The future is what I would be if I were not free and what I can have to be only because I am free."[113] Thus the future is what I have to be. The relation between my present and my future is an internal one. The meaning of my present activities is understood in the light of my project. "There is in my consciousness no moment which is not similarly defined by an internal relation to a future."[114] The future forms the attraction towards which I move. "Thus finality is rightly said to be *causality reversed*—that is, the efficacy of the future state."[115]

## THE EKSTATIC UNITY OF CONSCIOUSNESS

So far we have shown that the three temporal dimensions, viz. past, present and future are not discrete moments, but rather "structured moments" of an original "*ekstatic unity*." The three dimensions are related to one another in the form of internal relation. And the point of relation is the present which relates the past with the future. Thus original temporality of consciousness is conceived as a totality.

For Sartre, consciousness is a being which exists simultaneously in all its dimensions. "It is impossible to conceive of a consciousness which would not exist in these three dimensions."[116] This is to say that consciousness can at the same time fulfill these three requirements:

(I) to not-be what it is,

(2) to be what it is not, and

(3) to be what it is not and to not-be what it is.

It is "not what it is" in the sense that it is not identical with what it was in the past; and it "is what it is not" in the sense that it is not yet what it will be in the future. In this respect, consciousness is a being which is itself "outside itself"; that is, it is an "ambiguous" being.[117]

In this ekstatic temporality, the question of the unity of consciousness does not arise. This is because ekstatic unity is the inner structure of consciousness. Consciousness is not first a discrete instant which is to be unified afterwards; consciousness is always already a unity of past, present and future.

It should be remembered that, in *The Transcendence of the Ego*, Sartre, following Husserl, conceives consciousness as a discrete instant which is to be unified by acts of retention and protention.[118] In *Being and Nothingness* Sartre has abandoned this instantaneous conception of consciousness, saying that this conception fails to explain how the instants of consciousness are related to one another. The instant may be defined as an allegedly discrete segment of time, wholly distinct from prior and posterior moments.[119] It exists in the self-inclusion of identity—as a being-in-itself. In Sartre's ontology the in-itself is an isolated being which does not admit any forms of relation with what is not itself. Thus the relation between the instants is as inconceivable as the relation between the in-itselfs. Having no relation to prior and posterior moments, the instant is "non-temporal" and hence eternal. For Sartre, "eternity and the instant are here equivalent."[120] Being non-temporal, the instant cannot give rise to temporality which is succession by nature. For this reason Sartre rejects the instant "which is but one view of the mind." This view, says Sartre, is held by Husserl. He criticizes Husserl for not being able to "free himself from the instantaneous conception of consciousness."[121] If Husserl's conscious act is first given as instantaneous, then there is no way to get outside it. Each instant would be a self-enclosed being which is deprived of any means of relation to any other. Neither retention nor protention can bring about unification of the instants. As Sartre has pointed out:

> *"We saw in the preceding chapter how protentions batter in vain on the window-panes of the present without shattering them. The same goes for retentions... consciousness, as Husserl conceived it, cannot in reality transcend itself, either toward the world or toward the future or toward the past."*[122]

Having rejected the instantaneous conception of consciousness, Sartre proposes the conception of consciousness as ekstatic unity. And the continuous ekstasis of consciousness rules out the instant. Consciousness can exist simultaneously in the three ekstases of past, present and future because at the present it is nothingness. As a lack of being, consciousness is a "perpetual referring" to being outside itself. It refers itself back to what it was in the past and also projects itself toward what it will be in the future. At present consciousness is not. "As Present, Past and Future—all at the same time—the for-itself dispersing its being in three dimensions is temporal due to the very fact that it nihilates itself."[123] In other words, that consciousness exists in the ekstatic unity is possible because consciousness is freedom.[124]

## FREEDOM

So our inquiry into original temporality leads us to another structure of consciousness—freedom. According to Sartre, nihilation, temporalization, freedom and choice are one and the same thing.[125] We have said earlier that consciousness conditions the appearance of nothingness in the world. Consciousness, says Sartre, "has appeared to us as freedom." Here freedom is not a property subsisting in consciousness, but rather the inner structure of consciousness. "What we call freedom is impossible to distinguish from the being of 'human reality.' Man does not exist first in order to be free subsequently, there is no difference between the being of man and his being free." Freedom is the stuff of the being of man. "Man cannot be sometimes slave and sometimes free; he is wholly and forever free or he is not free at all."[126] Man is forever free, for *"man is condemned to be free."*[127]

Human reality is free because it can realize a nihilating rupture with the world and with itself; and this rupture is the same as freedom. "For the for-itself, to be is to nihilate the in-itself which it is."[128] This nihilating activity enables the for-itself to perpetually wrench away from itself, to break off with its own past, and to tear itself away from what it will be in the future. Thus the for-itself is free to the extent that it has to be its own nothingness in three dimensions: first, by temporalizing itself, which means that it does not allow itself to be determined by its own past; second, by rising up as consciousness of something and of itself, which indicates that nothing exists in consciousness; and finally, by being transcendence, i.e. a being which is originally a project, which is defined by its end.[129]

Since freedom has no essence, it cannot be defined. "It is freedom which is the foundation of all essences."[130] In freedom existence precedes essence. The past alone can be defined, what is happening in the present can merely be described. Freedom, though indefinable, is describable. Man learns his freedom through his action; hence freedom can be best understood by describing the structure of human actions.

The for-itself is the being which is defined by action. "Human reality does not exist first in order to act later, but for human reality, to be is to act and to cease to act is to cease to be."[131]

Action, as opposed to mere happening, is defined by intention.[132] The careless smoker who has through negligence caused the explosion of a powder magazine has not acted. Man is said to be acting only when he has an intention. By intention Sartre understands "a choice of the end."[133] This means that action, which entails intention, is a projection of the for-itself towards what it is not. As Sartre writes: "To conceive a project for the future, or form an intention, is to think of something which is not yet so, but which may be so."[134] Action is thus a project towards the end chosen. Freedom is the indispensable and fundamental condition of all action.[135]

The proponents of free will are concerned to find cases of decision for which there exists no prior cause, whereas the determinists contend that there is no action without cause. Sartre finds the two views unacceptable. Rejecting the theory of free will, Sartre says that every action is intentional; each action, therefore, has an end, and the end in turn is referred to a cause. To speak of an act without a cause is to speak of an act which would lack the intentional structure; and consequently the proponents of free will can only end up by rendering the act absurd. The determinists are accused by Sartre of stopping their investigation with the mere designation of the cause and motive. "The essential question," writes Sartre, "in fact lies beyond the complex organisation 'cause-intention-act-end'; indeed we ought to ask how a cause (or motive) can be constituted as such."[136] Sartre's contention is that actions do have causes but they are causes of a peculiar kind.

## CAUSE AND MOTIVE

According to Sartre, cause and motive can be regarded as a part of the action in so far as the for-itself confers on it values as cause or motive. They can be understood only in the light of an end which the for-itself chooses. If, for example, I accept a low-paying job it is because of fear; and fear is a motive. It is fear of dying from starvation. This fear is understood in relation to the value which I implicitly give to this life; that is, it is referred to the system of ideal objects of my projects. This means that cause and motive have meaning only within the ensemble of my projects. What is the difference between cause and motive?

By *cause* (*motif*) Sartre understands an objective appreciation of the situation. It is generally the reason for the act; that is, the ensemble of rational considerations which justify it. To explain this, Sartre takes an example from history. If Clovis, the first king of France, was converted to Catholicism it is because he saw an opportunity of getting into the good graces of the all powerful episcopate whose support would be necessary for the conquest of Gaul. Here the cause of Clovis' conversion is the political and religious state of Gaul and the relative strengths of the episcopate. It is an objective appreciation of the situation at that time. Sartre points out that this objective appreciation can be made only in the light of a presupposed end and within the limit of a project towards the end. In order for the power of the episcopate to appear objectively to Clovis as the cause of his conversion it is necessary first for him to posit as an end his rule on all of Gaul. If he had other ends, he would not see the situation of the episcopate as a cause; he would leave it in the state of 'unrevealed,' in a total obscurity. Thus the cause, far from determining an action, appears only in the light of a project towards an end.

In contrast, *motive* (*mobile*) is a subjective fact. "It is the ensemble of the desires, emotions and passions which urge me to accomplish a certain act."[137] The psychologists believe that motives are contained in the state of consciousness. They would interpret Clovis' conversion as a result of his ambition. And this ambition is regarded as a motive. Sartre's view is different from that of the psychologists. He says that there is no motive in consciousness because, as we saw, consciousness is contentless. For Sartre, "motives are only for consciousness."[138] From Sartre's view point, Clovis' ambition is not a quality contained in consciousness. "As it is not distinct from the project of conquering, we shall say that this first project of his possibilities in the light of which Clovis discovers a cause for being converted is precisely the motive."[139]

## THE UNDETERMINED CHOICE

Now it is clear that for Sartre neither cause nor motive can determine action in so far as action is defined by intention, i.e. a choice of an end. Cause and motive have meaning only within the compass of the project towards the end. "As soon as there are cause and motive ... there is already a positing of ends and consequently a choice."[140] "In fact, it is this original choice which originally *creates* all causes and motives which can guide us to partial actions."[141] It follows that *an action is free inasmuch as the original choice is free*: this is the real locus of Sartre's theory of freedom. Hence by freedom he means the undetermined choice. "Freedom is the freedom of choosing but not the freedom of not choosing."[142] For the for-itself, to be is to choose itself.[143] Sartre writes:

> *"Every for itself is* a free choice; *each of its acts—the most insignificant as well as the most weighty—expresses this choice and emanates from it. This is what we have called our freedom."*[144]

The for-itself is a choice because it is defined ontologically as a lack. "The for-itself chooses because it is lack; freedom is really synonymous with lack."[145] What the for-itself lacks is the being-in-itself. The for-itself never wants to remain a lack; it desires to unite itself with the in-itself. The unity, if realized, would be called the being-in-itself-for-itself. The original choice of the for-itself is the choice of itself as being united with the in-itself. The unity is the ideal of the for-itself. Its fundamental project aims at realizing this ideal. And the "secondary" projects which aim at realization of a particular goal of the for-itself are based on the fundamental project.

Thus all action expresses a choice of the end. The action is not limited to itself; it refers immediately to the end chosen. And the end lies in the future. It should be noted here that Freud, unlike Sartre, thinks that the determinants of human actions derive their forces from the past, not from the future. According to Freud, action is symbolic because it expresses an underlying desire which itself would manifest a more profound complex. The complexes are constituted by the subject's historical situation. For example, it is the child's situation in the family that determines in him the birth of the Oedipus complex. Such a complex, retained in the unconscious, comes out from time to time to motivate the subject's action. In this sense, human action cannot be totally free because it is determined by the impulses emanating from the unconscious. Sartre, therefore, regards Freud's theory as psychic determinism. Sartre criticizes Freud for giving too much importance to the past dimension of men. "The dimension of the future," writes Sartre, "does not exist for psychoanalysis."[146] Human reality in the Freudian theory loses one of its ekstases and can be interpreted solely by a regression towards the past from the stand-point of the present. Sartre notes that instead of understanding the action in terms of the past as Freud did, we can conceive of it as turning back of the future towards the present. Each action manifests the project towards the end in the future. The inferiority complex, for example, is not a product of my past but rather "a project of my own for-itself in the world in the presence of the other."[147] As such it is always transcendence; it is a way of choosing myself. "It is impossible seriously to consider the feeling of inferiority without determining it in terms of the future and of my possibilities."[148] Hence every action, no matter how trivial, is not the simple effect of the prior psychic state but rather it "is integrated as secondary structure in global structures and finally in the totality which I am."[149]

It may be argued from the Freudian viewpoint that if it is the case that all action refers to the original choice, it is possible that a choice which has been made in the past still motivates the action in the present; and consequently the action expresses the choice made in the past. To this, Sartre would reply that the original choice is always renewed; as such there is no question of its motivating the action from the past. The fundamental project, since it is perpetually renewed, is coextensive with the entire life of consciousness.

> *"Since freedom is a being-without-support and without-a-spring-board, the project in order to be must be constantly renewed. I choose myself perpetually and can never be merely by virtue of having-been-chosen; otherwise I should fall into the pure and simple existence of the in-itself."*[150]

Since the choice is coextensive with the whole life of consciousness, consciousness cannot stop choosing; to be conscious is to choose. *Consciousness and choice are one and the same thing.*[151] Sartre rules out the possibility of the unconscious choice, because choice, being identical with consciousness, must of necessity be non-thetic consciousness of choice.

Consciousness, therefore, is free choice. Choice is said to be absurd, not because it is without reasons, but because it is beyond reasons. It is by choice that "all foundations and all reasons come into being."[152] This is to say that freedom is a choice of its being but not the foundation of its being. If it were its own foundation, it would be necessary that freedom should decide its being-free; that is, it should be a choice of itself as freedom. If freedom were to choose its being-free, this would suppose that the possibility of being-free and the possibility of not being free exist equally before the free choice of freedom. Since to choose between the two alternatives presupposes another prior freedom which would choose being-free, this would lead to infinite regress. "In fact, we are a freedom which chooses, but we do not choose to be free. We are condemned to freedom, as we said earlier, thrown into freedom or, as Heidegger says, 'abandoned.'"[153] Human reality is 'condemned' to freedom because it does not choose to be free. Nor can it stop choosing. This is because "not to choose is, in fact, to choose not to choose."[154] Even suicide is a choice and affirmation of being.[155] So human reality "is not free not to exist or not to be free."[156]

## FACTICITY OF FREEDOM

Freedom is "total and infinite." Sartre rejects all forms of determinism. He then tries to cope with the classical arguments against absolute freedom. The determinists say that man is not free because he is subject to hereditary and environmental pressures. His freedom is limited by his family, nationality, language, sex, etc. Man seems to encounter resistance and obstacle everywhere. To these objections, Sartre replies, first of all, that freedom does not mean the ability to obtain what one has wished. "In other words success is not important to freedom."[157] The philosophical notion of freedom, which Sartre accepts, means only "the autonomy of choice."[158] It is true that there is certain given datum which prevents full exercise of freedom. Nevertheless the resistance is not a limit to freedom but rather a necessary condition for its appearance. "There can be a free for-itself only as engaged in a resisting world. Outside of this engagement the notions of freedom, of determinism, of necessity lose all meaning."[159] The given in itself does not restrain freedom; it is neutral. Just as cause and motive are constituted as such only within the compass of the end, so also the given is revealed as resistance or as aid only in the light of human projects. The rock, for example, can show its resistance only to the mountaineer who makes a project of scaling. For the simple tourist whose project is a pure aesthetic appreciation of the landscape, the rock is not revealed either as scalable or as not-scalable; it is either beautiful or ugly.

The given is a part of facticity of freedom. By facticity Sartre means "the given which it (freedom) has to be and which it illuminates by its project."[160] And the synthetic organization of facticity illuminated by freedom constitutes 'situation.' To choose is to choose in situation. Man, therefore, is called "being-in-situation."[161] Sartre writes: "There is freedom only in a situation and there is a situation only through freedom."[162] There are five structural aspects of the situation: my place, my past, my environment, my fellowmen, and my death.

### A. My Place

"My place" is the present place I live in. It presupposes different places in which I lived going back to the place of my birth.

It is from this original place that I shift to other places. The determinist says that the choice of one place excludes the choice of other places. Sartre points out that freedom can exist only in restricted form since freedom is choice. Every choice implies elimination and selection; that is, every choice is a choice of finitude. "Thus freedom can be truly free only by constituting facticity as its own restriction."[163] Some may say that the occupation of a place restricts my freedom of travelling; I am not free to go to Chicago because of the fact that I am a minor government official at Bangkok. According to Sartre, place in itself is neutral. It is revealed as an obstacle or as a help only in the light of my project towards a certain end. "Thus our freedom itself creates the obstacles from which we suffer."[164] It is freedom which causes our place to appear as a resistance by positing its end.

**B. My Past**

My past is what I have been. In so far as I exist, I cannot lack having a past. The for-itself "comes into the world with a past."[165] "Our acts," says the proverb, "follow after us." Does this mean that the past determines my action? It appears to the determinists that man is not free because his present existence is determined and influenced by his past. This view is not acceptable to Sartre. According to him, the past is perpetually 'in suspense,' because I can freely give a new meaning to it. And the meaning I give depends upon my present project. "By projecting myself towards my ends, I preserve the past with me, and by action I decide its meaning."[166] Hence it is my choice of the future goal that decides the meaning of my past. And it is within the compass of my project that the past is manifested as the motivation of my present action. As Sartre has pointed out:

> *"Thus like place, the past is integrated with the situation when the for-itself by its choice of future confers on its past facticity a value in terms of which this facticity motivates the act and conduct of the for-itself."*[167]

## C. My Environment

My environments (*entours*) are not the place which I occupy but the instrumental things which surround me with their coefficients of adversity and utility. They are tools which have their value and resistance. The synthetic organization of the tools constitutes the unity of my *Umwelt*, and this *Umwelt* can be revealed only within the limits of a free project.[168] A tool is in itself indifferent; it offers neither help nor resistance. It is only within my project that the tool becomes my adversity or utility. Suppose I wish to arrive at the next town as quickly as possible and I plan to go there by bicycle. Since the bicycle has a flat tire, it offers resistance. This bicycle is revealed as resistance because I have chosen it for a ride; it is included in my project. This illustration shows that "the adversity of things and their potentialities in general are illuminated by the end chosen."[169] Thus Sartre's position regarding environments is the same as that of place; both are neutral, it is my free project which makes them an aid or a resistance.

## D. My Fellowmen

It is not by me alone that meanings come to instrumental things. Living in the world, I encounter my fellowmen who also put meanings into things. I find myself engaged in an already meaningful world which reflects to me meanings which my free project has not given to them. I come across instruction, directions, orders, prohibitions which are addressed to me and which I have to obey if I do not want to take the wrong street, to miss the train, to be arrested, etc. My freedom seems to be limited by the existence of the Other. Moreover, through the Other arise certain determinations which I am without having chosen; that is, for the Other I am Asian, rich, ugly, etc. Thus the true limit of my freedom lies in the fact that the Other apprehends me as the Other-as-object, and that my situation becomes for him an objective form.[170] These two characteristic limits represent the boundaries of my freedom. Sartre, however, points out that by my free recognition of the Other's freedom I recover my being-as-object. If, on the contrary, I consider the Other as pure object, then all determinations from the Other disappear immediately. Since "I can apprehend the Other as a freedom only within the free project of apprehending him as such," it is nothing but my freedom which allows the Other's freedom to impose limit on it. Sartre, therefore, admits that there is limit of freedom—the limit which comes from freedom itself. "Just as thought according to Spinoza can be limited only by thought, so freedom can be limited only by freedom."[171]

## E. My Death

The realists consider death as a door opening upon the nothingness of human reality, as something non-human. This realistic conception of death is not acceptable to Sartre who regards death as a human phenomenon. "It is the phenomenon of my personal life which makes of this life a unique life—that is, a life which does not begin again, a life in which one never recovers his stroke." Heidegger also accepts this humanization of death and defines *Dasein* as being-towards-death (*Sein-zum-Tode*).[172] "Thus death reveals itself as that possibility which is one's ownmost."[173] Death is for *Dasein* the capital possibility from which all other possibilities derive their status. Unlike Heidegger, Sartre does not consider death to be a possibility of the for-itself. For him death is "the nihilation of all my possibilities."[174] Death as the external limit of life does not make limit of my freedom. "The freedom which is my freedom remains total and infinite. Death is not an obstacle to my projects; it is only a destiny of these projects elsewhere." Death is the external limit which the for-itself will never encounter for when death is there, the for-itself is no longer there.

## RESPONSIBILITY

It is clear from the foregoing discussion that situation is not a limit to freedom, but rather a necessary condition for the appearance of freedom. Without limit, freedom is absolute. What necessarily follows from absolute freedom is responsibility. By responsibility Sartre simply means "consciousness (of) being the incontestable author of an event or of an object." I am responsible for giving meanings to things, i.e. for being the "author" of the situation, the world and the value. In fact, I am responsible for all things except for my responsibility, because I am not the foundation of my being. Sartre writes:

> *"Therefore everything takes place as if I were compelled to be responsible. I am abandoned in the world ... in the sense that I find myself suddenly alone and without help, engaged in a world for which I bear the whole responsibility without being able, whatever I do, to tear myself away from this responsibility for an instant."*[175]

It is precisely this constant awareness of responsibility that plunges the for-itself into anguish.

## ANGUISH

Anguish of the for-itself is anxiety resulting from the awareness of itself as freedom. Since it is nothingness, the for-itself cannot appeal to any *a priori* "human nature" for guidance in making a choice. Finding itself alone and without help, it feels insecure and anxious. According to Sartre, anguish is different from fear. "A situation provokes *fear* if there is a possibility of my life being changed from without; my being provokes *anguish* to the extent that I distrust myself and my own reactions in that situation." In other words, fear is unreflective apprehension of the transcendent object as a danger for me whereas anguish is reflective apprehension of myself as freedom. That is why Sartre says that "anguish is born as a structure of the reflective consciousness"[176] and that "it is in anguish that man gets the consciousness of his freedom." According to Sartre, there are three kinds of anguish: anguish in the face of the future, anguish in the face of the past and ethical anguish.

First, *anguish in the face of the future* is "precisely my consciousness of being my own future, in the mode of not-being." In this sense I am in anguish because I am aware that my present being cannot determine my action in the future. What I will do is a mere possibility. Anguish arises when I recognize a possibility as my possibility and see myself separated from the future. For example, walking on a narrow path along a precipice, I feel anguish at the thought that I may possibly throw myself over the precipice at any time and nothing prevents me from doing such a thing. Here anguish implies the apprehension of throwing myself over the precipice as "my" possibility.

Secondly, *anguish in the face of the past* arises because "man is always separated by a nothingness from his essence."[177] Essence is all that human reality apprehends in itself as having been. Man is in anguish because he realizes that what he was cannot determine what he is. Included in this type is the anguish of the gambler who has freely and sincerely decided not to gamble any more and who, on approaching the gaming table, suddenly sees the total inefficacy of the past solution. He perceives with anguish that nothing prevents him from gambling.

Finally, everyday morality is not exclusive of *ethical anguish*. There is ethical anguish when I consider myself in my original relation to values. For Sartre, values do not have real being, "for every value which would base its ideal nature on its being would thereby cease even to be a value." Value is beyond being.[178] I am *"a being by whom values exist."*[179] And I feel anguish because nothing justifies adopting this or that particular value or scale of values. "My freedom is anguished at being the foundation of values while itself without foundation."[180]

## BAD FAITH

Man is hardly in pure anguish because most of the time he flees anguish in bad faith (*mauvaise foi*). Thus bad faith is the attempt to flee anguish. It is described as self-deception or a lie to oneself,[181] for it tries to hide freedom from oneself. Bad faith is an attitude of excuses, i.e. a refusal to recognize what I am, namely, a being who is both facticity *and* transcendence. "These two aspects of human reality are and ought to be capable of a valid coordination. But bad faith does not wish either to coordinate them or to surmount them in a synthesis." These statements indicate that bad faith does not solely consist in the denial of one's transcendence in order to flee anguish; it also consists in the denial of one's facticity and overemphasis on one's transcendence.

In the case of the denial of transcendences, a man of bad faith looks at himself as a thing, an in-itself. What Sartre calls *"the spirit of seriousness"*[182] may be regarded as a typical example of bad faith of this kind. Man is serious when he takes himself for a thing, i.e. a being-in-the-midst-of-the-world. The serious man is "of the world" and never imagines the possibility of getting out of it, for he has given to himself the type of existence of the rock. For Sartre the materialists are revolutionaries because they apprehend themselves in terms of the world which oppresses them and they want to change this world. So the revolutionaries are serious. "Marx proposed the original dogma of the serious when he asserted the priority of object over subject."[183] By taking himself for a thing, the serious man overemphasizes his facticity while denying his transcendence; he is in bad faith.

Man is in another type of bad faith if he overemphasizes his transcendence and denies his facticity; that is, if he looks upon himself as pure freedom without commitment and responsibility. His freedom remains aloof and independent; it is an empty, detached freedom. In contrast with the serious man who sinks into the world in seriousness, the man of pure freedom tries to flee from the world. Orestes, the hero in *The Flies,* is in bad faith of this kind. He commits a crime without guilt or anguish. He asserts that "I am free. Beyond anguish, beyond remorse."[184] Moreover, Orestes spurns Zeus' offer of the throne of Argos in exchange for repudiation of his crime; he wants to remain detached even in his new-found situated freedom. His ideal of freedom appears to be self-defeated because, as Sartre says, outside the situation the notion of freedom loses all meaning.[185] According to Sartre, it is not possible for man to flee from the world. *"We in no case get out of an existing world."*[186] To regard oneself as being totally detached from the world is to be in bad faith.

That one flees anguish in bad faith is a fact of life; it is a type of being in the world. It is neither good nor bad in itself. Sartre, however, goes beyond his phenomenological description in making a value judgement that the being of the man of bad faith is "corrupted."[187] Sartre's evaluative analysis is shown by his blunt condemnation of the "cowards" who hide from themselves their total freedom either in the spirit of seriousness or by deterministic excuses.[188] This evaluative analysis makes Sartre enter the sphere of what is known as existentialist ethics, for his description becomes a "moral description."[189] In Sartre's ethics, freedom is regarded as the goal of man's life; it is the end in itself. Sartre says:

> *"Furthermore I can pronounce a moral judgement. For I declare that freedom, in respect of concrete circumstances, can have no other end and aim but itself; and when once a man has seen that values depend upon himself in that state of forsakenness he can will only one thing, and that is freedom as foundation of all values."*[190]

Man wills "freedom for freedom's sake." As such, man should liberate himself from bad faith in order to re-discover his hidden freedom. But the question is: How can man escape bad faith? It is said that man of bad faith is hiding the truth from himself, he is not sincere to himself. Is it possible for man to escape bad faith by practising sincerity?

"To be sincere," writes Sartre, "is to be what one is."[191] A sincere man is believed to be a kind of person who, if he is cowardly, admits that he is a coward. "It is necessary that a man be for himself only what he is."[192] But to be what one is is to be a thing, an in-itself. The nature of man is to not-be what he is and to be what he is not. Thus man cannot be what he is, and thereby the ideal of sincerity is not possible to achieve because it goes against the nature of human reality. If man insists on determining exactly what he is, then he is constituting himself as a thing. As a result, he ends up in bad faith. Hence, sincerity is itself in bad faith. Sincerity is not possible because man cannot be what he is. If man could be what he is, then bad faith would not be possible. "Thus in order for bad faith to be possible, sincerity itself must be in bad faith."[193]

## GOOD FAITH

Man, therefore, cannot escape bad faith by practising sincerity. Being in bad faith, man has a very rare chance for escape. As Sartre himself has pointed out: "Once this mode of being has been realized, it is as difficult to get out of it as to wake oneself up; bad faith is a type of being in the world, like waking or dreaming, which by itself tends to perpetuate itself."[194] This does not mean that bad faith is inescapable. According to Sartre, man can escape bad faith by a "*radical conversion.*" The radical conversion supposes "a self-recovery of being which was previously corrupted."[195] This self-recovery Sartre calls "*authenticity*" or "*good faith.*"[196] What would good faith be like? We have already seen that bad faith is a refusal to recognize that man is both facticity and transcendence. As opposed to this, good faith would be a "valid coordination" of facticity and transcendence. The man of good faith is always aware that he is a freedom-in-situation. He neither sinks into the world in seriousness nor flees from it through total detachment. He takes freedom to be the goal of his actions. Sartre writes: "The actions of men of good faith have, as their ultimate significance, the quest of freedom itself as such."[197] The man of good faith is aware that he is the being by whom values exist. In making a choice, he feels anguish because he knows that "nothing, absolutely nothing, justifies me in adopting this or that particular value, this or that scale of values."[198] Sartre portrays a man of good faith in several of his literary writings. For example, in *The Age of Reason*, Sartre says of Mathieu:

> *"He could do what he liked, no one had the right to advise him, there would be for him no Good nor Evil unless he brought them into being ... He was ... free and alone, without assistance and without*

*excuse, condemned to decide without support from any quarter, condemned for ever to be free."*[199]

And in *The Devil and The Good Lord,* Goetz says:

> *"There was no one but myself; I alone decided on Evil; and I alone invented Good. It was I who cheated, I who worked miracles, I who accused myself today, I alone who can absolve myself; I, man.* If God exists, man is nothing; if man exists ... God doesn't exist."[200]

## SARTREAN ETHICS

It is clear from the foregoing discussion that in the sphere of ethics Sartre is a subjectivist because he maintains that good and evil are invented by man. Sartre rejects the existence of fixed, objective values and moral principles. According to him, man cannot have recourse to any moral principles for guidance; he has to invent them for himself. The suggestion that Sartre can give to a person who is in moral perplexity is that "you are free, therefore choose—that is to say, invent." Nothing tells man what to choose. "One can choose anything, but only if it is upon the plane of free commitment." Thus free choice is the foundation of morality. Once one makes a free choice, there is no possibility of a moral mistake. Whatever I choose is right for me. "Whenever a man chooses his purpose and his commitment in all clearness and in all sincerity, whatever that purpose may be, it is impossible to prefer another for him." This position creates one difficulty. If man can never be wrong in making a free choice, he can never be right, since these notions are interrelated. And if man can be neither right nor wrong, how can he be praised or blamed, and how can he be responsible?

## DESIRE

In Sartre's ethics, freedom is regarded as the goal of all actions. Freedom, however, is not the ideal which man desires to realize. Fundamentally man is the desire to be.[201] Desire is defined as "a lack of being." In this respect, desire has its root in the nothingness of human reality. Being a void or emptiness, human reality wants to fill itself with the full positivity of the in-itself; that is, it desires to be the in-itself-for-itself. The ideal is to be identified with the in-itself and yet to remain as free consciousness. This ideal is unrealizable because all identification with the in-itself requires the disappearance of consciousness. Hence human reality has desired to realize the unrealizable ideal: And in every case of desire there is frustration. *"Man is useless passion."*[202] This passion is a cause of man's suffering. "Human reality therefore is by nature an unhappy consciousness with no possibility of surpassing its unhappy state."

There is no possibility of cessation of suffering because desire is neither satiable nor destructible. Desire cannot be got rid of for the reason that it is the inner structure of consciousness. To be conscious is to desire the in-itself. Thus the destruction of desire requires the extinction of consciousness. Where there is consciousness, there is desire. Such a desire manifests itself in several concrete forms such as jealousy, greed, courage, love of art, etc., but all of them are reducible to either a *desire to be* or a *desire to have.* "Ultimately a desire can be only the desire to be or the desire to have."[203] The latter expresses itself in the form of an appropriation or possession. It is by the appropriation of objects that the project to have aims at realizing the same value as the desire to be. The appropriation "is nothing save the symbol of the ideal of the for-itself or value." Through the appropriation human reality tries to unite itself with the in-itself.

> *"Possession is a magical relation; I am those objects which I possess, but outside, so to speak, facing myself, I create them as independent of me; what I possess is mine outside me ... without it I am nothing save a nothingness which possesses ..."*[204]

Thus the desire to have and the desire to be have the same goal, i.e. the identification of the for-itself with the in-itself. That is why they are inseparable. "It is impossible to find a desire to be which is not accompanied by a desire to have, and conversely."[205]

Desiring to be the in-itself-for-itself, man performs action. As such, the desire to be seems to be the driving force of human action. Man does not choose his ideal, for there is no other ideal to be chosen except the in-itself-for-itself. Every choice presupposes alternatives, but in the case of the ideal there are none. Man is not free not to choose his ideal, for he is under the compulsion of the desire to be. In this respect, Sartre's libertarianism is logically posterior to the desire to be: *man chooses, not the ultimate end, but merely the means thereto.* Sartre, therefore, is a libertarian with respect to the means, and a determinist with respect to the end. Nevertheless the end, unlike the Unmoved Mover of Aristotle, does not exercise over man an attraction from outside, it is not the external cause. The relation between man and his ideal is an internal one. The ideal is what man has to be. He projects himself towards it in order to fulfill his desire. Here we find that the desire is the cause of man's search for completeness which is the unrealizable ideal. Since the search is bound to end up in frustration, the desire to be is the cause of man's suffering. Sartre's ethics offers no remedy for such a suffering.

## A SUMMARY

So far we have considered in some detail Sartre's conception of consciousness. Now we shall summarize what emerges from the foregoing discussions.

Consciousness is defined by intentionality; all consciousness is a revealing intuition of something. Emptied of all egological structure, consciousness is contentless; neither object nor image is in consciousness. Since all being is on the side of the object, consciousness is a total emptiness or nothingness. The being of consciousness is called the for-itself which is described as "being what it is not, and not being what it is." It is a negation of the being of the object or the in-itself which is "what it is." Although it is a lack of being, consciousness 'exists' as a pure appearance to the extent that it is implicitly conscious of itself whenever it is positionally conscious of the object. This is to say that consciousness 'is' in the mode of self-consciousness or self transparency. Thus, consciousness is necessarily self-conscious. Consciousness is temporal; it has being outside of it, before and behind. Before itself, it has to be its future; and behind itself, it has to be its past. At present it is not what it is (past) and it is what it is not (future). Its being is therefore ambiguous. Consciousness is not instantaneous; it is an ekstatic unity of past, present and future. And consciousness can exist simultaneously in the three dimensions because it is freedom. Freedom here is used in the sense of spontaneity and undetermined choice. Being aware of its own freedom, consciousness feels anguish and tries to flee it by putting itself in bad faith. As a lack of being, consciousness desires to fill itself with the in-itself. Its ideal is to be the in-itself-for-itself. But this ideal is unrealizable. Its desire becomes a useless passion. Being unable to realize its ideal, consciousness is subject to constant frustration and suffering; it is unhappy consciousness with no possibility of surpassing its unhappy state.

## A REVIEW OF NOTHINGNESS

In retrospect, we find that nothingness is one of the most important concepts of Sartre's consciousness. Without referring to nothingness, Sartre cannot account for the notions of freedom, temporality and desire. As we have already seen, consciousness is freedom because it does not belong to the causal order of the world; it is *not anything* in the world. Consciousness can exist simultaneously in the dimensions of past, present and future because at present it *is not* and has to be its past and its future. And finally, consciousness is the desire to be since it is a lack of being, i.e. nothingness. Having seen how the notion of nothingness is closely tied with the other three notions, we are not surprised to find this statement in *Being and Nothingness*: "Freedom, choice, nihilation, temporalization are all one and the same thing."[206] Thus the conception of consciousness as nothingness may be regarded as a 'premise' which provides justification for the other notions of consciousness. The title of the book, *Being and Nothingness,* bears testimony of the significance of this conception. If the notion of nothingness is rejected, then the other notions related to it will lose their ground. The question now is: Can the conception of consciousness as nothingness be justifiable in Sartre's own framework?

From Sartre's viewpoint, the reality of nothingness is justified only when it can be described by phenomenological descriptions, i.e. when it is given to our intuition. Sartre does not explain how nothingness is given to intuition. What he says is: "It is necessary that *in some way* Nothingness be given."[207] But in what way? We tend to think that nothingness is in no way given to intuition. If consciousness were nothingness, its non-being would not be given to phenomenological reflection. This is because consciousness is consciousness of *something,* it cannot be consciousness of *nothing*. Hence the reality of nothingness cannot be described by phenomenological description.

To do justice to Sartre, one may say that consciousness does not posit nothingness as its object, rather it is implicitly aware of nothingness in the mode of self-consciousness. Being aware of something, consciousness is aware of itself as *not being* that thing. It is in this way that consciousness is aware of its own nothingness. In this sense nothingness means "no-thing" or not-being-this-thing. It is similar to the Platonic notion of 'otherness.' In the *Sophist,* Plato says that 'what-is-not' is identified with otherness.[208] Sartre, following Plato, maintains that nothingness means a "being-other-than-object." "To be other than being," writes Sartre, "is to be self-conscious in the unity of the temporalizing ekstases... For the only way in which the other can exist as other is to be consciousness (of) being other."[209]

This interpretation of nothingness creates one difficulty. If nothingness simply means "being-other-than-object," then nothingness is not a negation of being. This is because otherness does not imply non-being. "That which is not" is said to mean "not something contrary to what exists but only something different."[210] The different is simply "the not so-and-so"—anything that exists but is defined negatively as different from something else. Thus what is not a book is not a non-being, but merely something else; and just the fact that consciousness is not its object does not necessarily imply that consciousness is a non-being. In *The Tragic Finale,*[211] Wilfrid Desan remarks that in the *tabula rasa* conception of mind one can speak of mind as nothingness in the sense of potentiality which by knowing can become anything; it is nothingness in the sense that it is not yet what it will know. It is not a non-being in its own structure. Yet, in order to grasp what it is not, it ought to be a nature different from its 'material' object and may therefore be characterized as immaterial.

In spite of all this difficulty, Sartre maintains that consciousness is nothingness in the sense of non-being. He gives all being to the object and eliminates all positivity from consciousness. By throwing the whole being into the in-itself, Sartre makes consciousness empty and vacant. Yet it has several activities to perform; worldliness, spatiality, quantity, values, instrumentality, temporality—all come into being through the activities of consciousness. Thus consciousness may be described as activity despite vacuity. In an aptly turned phrase, Wilfrid Desan has remarked that the Sartrean consciousness *"has nothing to be and all to do."*[212] The question now is: Can a consciousness which is a non-being have energy for performing activities? We think that non-being can neither act nor think. To think is to be. In order to perform its activities, consciousness must exist.

Sartre, however, arrives at the conclusion that consciousness is nothingness after he has removed all the contents, especially the transcendental ego, out of it. Without the ego, consciousness is contentless and thereby nothingness. It appears to us that Sartre's conception of consciousness as nothingness is the necessary outcome of his rejection of the transcendental ego. By taking consciousness to be nothingness, Sartre is able to differentiate the being-for-itself from the being-in-itself. In fact, Sartre's phenomenological ontology can stand only when the transcendental ego is rejected; that is, when all being is put on the side of the object and consciousness is nothing. Consciousness then is established as a revealing intuition of being. Through phenomenological description of consciousness, Sartre discovers the realm of being. He offers the phenomenological theory of being as a negated unity—a totality detotalized by the nihilating activity of consciousness.

Thus Sartre's rejection of the transcendental ego is a prerequisite condition for the possibility of his ontology. Just as Husserl finds it necessary to introduce the transcendental ego if he wants to characterize the phenomenological sphere, so also Sartre finds it necessary to reject the transcendental ego if he wants to establish his phenomenological ontology. Sartre's purpose in rejecting the ego is different from that of the early Buddhist who rejects the permanent self or *ātman* for both theoretical and practical purposes. How does the Buddhist reject the self? Is that self the same as Husserl's transcendental ego? We shall try to answer these and other questions in the next chapter.

## NOTES

1 Sartre, J-P., "Consciousness of Self and Knowledge of Self", N. Lawrence and D O'Connor (eds.), *Readings in Existential Phenomenology,* Prentice-Hall, 1967, p. 124.
2 Sartre, J-P., *The Transcendence of the Ego,* tr. by F. Williams and R. Kirkpatrick, Noonday Press, 1959, p. 38.
3 Sartre, J-P., *Imagination: A Psychological Critique,* tr. by F. Williams, The University of Michigan Press, 1972, p. 146.
4 TE. 40-42.
5 TE. 21, 98.
6 Sartre, J-P., *Imagination: A Psychological Critique,* p. 115.
7 Sartre, J-P., *The Psychology of Imagination,* tr. by B. Frechtman, Methuen, 1972, p. 27.
8 TE. 98-9.
9 Sartre, J-P., *Being and Nothingness,* tr. by Hazel E. Barnes, Pocket Books, New York, 1966, p. 16n.
10 TE. 100.
11 TE. 42; BN. 17.
12 BN. 786.
13 BN. 725.
14 BN. 17.

15 BN 14.
16 TE. 40.
17 BN 787.
18 BN. 12.
19 TE. 40.
20 BN. 15.
21 BN. 11.
22 BN. 12.
23 Danto, A.C., *Sartre,* Fontana, 1979, p. 59.
24 BN. 11.
25 BN. 12.
26 TE. 47.
27 TE. 44, BN. 11.
28 BN. 579.
29 BN. 23, 786.
30 BN. 790.
31 BN. 650.
32 BN. 23-4.
33 BN. 23.
34 BN. 9.
35 Husserl B. *Ideas,* tr. by W.R. Boyce Gibson, George Allen & Unwin, 1969, s. 98, p. 287.
36 BN. 318.
37 BN. 21.
38 BN. 722.
39 Sartre, J-P., *Imagination: A Psychological Critique,* p. 116 .
40 BN. 25.
41 The subtitle of *L'être et le Néant* is "essai d'ontologie phénoménologique."
42 BN. 785.
43 Heidegger, M., *Being and Time,* tr. by John Macquarrie and Edward Robinson, Basil Blackwell, 1978, p. 62.
44 BN. 29.
45 BN. 29.
46 BN. 28.
47 BN. 17.
48 BN. 723.
49 BN. 786.
50 BN. 786.
51 BN. 217.
52 BN. 252.
53 BN. 116.
54 BN. 19.
55 BN. 86.
56 BN. 172.
57 BN. 17.
58 BN. 786.

59 BN. 49.
60 BN. 786.
61 BN. 790.
62 BN. 791.
63 BN. 36.
64 BN. 37.
65 BN. 43.
66 BN. 38.
67 BN. 42.
68 BN. 42.
69 BN. 42.
70 BN. 40.
71 BN. 56.
72 BN. 56.
73 BN. 55.
74 BN. 121.
75 BN. 57.
76 BN. 59.
77 BN. 57-8.
78 BN. 138, 567.
79 BN. 40.
80 BN. 176.
81 BN. 29.
82 BN. 202.
83 BN. 223.
84 BN. 222.
85 BN. 159.
86 BN. 28-9.
87 BN. 203.
88 BN. 190.
89 BN. 159.
90 BN. 163.
91 BN. 168.
92 BN. 64.
93 BN. 174.
94 BN. 172.
95 BN. 207.
96 BN. 179.
97 BN. 197.
98 BN. 197.
99 BN. 175.
100 BN. 725.
101 BN. 177.
102 BN. 179.
103 BN. 179.
104 BN. 221.
105 BN. 201.

106 BN. 179.
107 BN. 182.
108 BN. 139.
109 BN. 138.
110 BN. 52.
111 BN. 185.
112 BN. 147.
113 BN. 186.
114 BN. 181-2.
115 BN. 182.
116 BN. 197.
117 BN. 196.
118 BN. 145 n.
119 See above, pp 29-30
120 Fell, J.P., *Heidegger and Sartre,* Columbia University Press, New York, 1979, p. 31.
121 BN. 190.
122 BN. 599.
123 BN. 162.
124 BN. 202.
125 Bhadra, M.K., *A Critical Study of Sartre's Ontology of Consciousness,* The University of Burdwan, 1976, p. 129.
126 BN. 599.
127 BN. 60.
128 BN. 60.
129 BN. 569.
130 Sartre, J-P., *Existentialism and Humanism,* tr. by P. Mairet, Eyre Methuen, London, 1980, p. 34.
131 BN. 567.
132 BN. 584.
133 BN. 566.
134 BN. 613.
135 BN. 613.
136 BN. 614.
137 Warnock, M., *The Philosophy of Sartre,* Hutchinson University Library, 1972, p. 113.
138 BN. 563.
139 BN. 564.
140 BN. 576.
141 BN. 71.
142 BN. 578-9.
143 BN. 594.
144 BN. 598.
145 BN. 618-9.
146 BN. 568.
147 BN. 764.
148 BN. 722.

149 BN. 590.
150 BN. 591.
151 BN. 592.
152 BN. 591.
153 BN. 617.
154 BN. 595.
155 BN. 616.
156 BN. 623.
157 BN. 619.
158 BN. 616.
159 BN. 625.
160 BN. 621.
161 BN. 622.
162 BN. 621.
163 BN. 629.
164 BN. 701.
165 BN. 629.
166 BN. 636.
167 BN. 635.
168 BN. 197.
169 BN. 640.
170 BN. 647.
171 BN. 648.
172 BN. 652.
173 BN. 672.
174 BN. 674.
175 BN. 673.
176 BN. 682.
177 Heidegger, M., op.cit., p. 277.
178 Ibid. p. 294.
179 BN. 687.
180 BN. 700.
181 BN. 707.
182 BN. 710.
183 BN. 65.
184 BN. 78.
185 BN. 65.
186 BN. 68.
187 BN. 72.
188 BN. 76.
189 BN. 143.
190 BN. 76.
191 BN. 76.
192 BN. 87.
193 BN. 98.
194 BN. 740, 796.
195 BN. 741.

196 Sartre, J-P., *Three Plays: Altona, Men Without Shadows, The Flies,* Penguin Books, 1981, p. 303.
197 BN. 621.
198 BN (Philosophical Library, New York, p. 56), p. 312.
199 BN. 116n.
200 Sartre, J-P., *Existentialism and Humanism,* p. 52.
201 BN. 796.
202 *Existentialism and Humanism,* p. 51.
203 BN. 105.
204 BN. 100-101.
205 BN. 112.
206 BN. 113.
207 BN. 116n.
208 BN. 116n.
209 *Existentialism and Humanism,* p. 51.
210 BN. 76.
211 Sartre, J-P., *The Age of Reason,* tr. by Eric Sutton, Penguin Books, 1982, pp. 242-3.
212 Sartre, J-P; *The Devil and The Good Lord and Two Other Plays,* Vintage Books, 1960, p.141.
213 *Existentialism and Humanism,* p.38.
214 Ibid., p. 54.
215 Ibid., p. 50.
216 BN. 722.
217 BN. 735.
218 BN. 784.
219 BN. 140.
220 BN. 742.
221 BN. 755.
222 BN. 755.
223 BN. 763.
224 BN. 599.
225 BN. 56..
226 Plato, *Sophist,* 257b.
227 BN. 787.
228 Cornford, F. M., *Plato and Parmenides,* Routledge and Kegan Paul, 1950, p. 231.
229 Desan, W., *The Tragic Finale,* Harvard University Press, 1954.
230 Desan, W., op.cit., p. 56.

# PART TWO
# SELFLESSNESS IN EARLY BUDDHISM

# III

# THE BUDDHIST'S REJECTION OF THE SELF

In directing our attention to the field of Indian philosophy, we find that the Buddhist doctrine of *anattā* bears some re semblance to Sartre's non-egological treatment of consciousness. The theory of *anattā* (Sanskrit, *nairātmyavāda*) first appeared in the Buddha's second sermon called *Anattalakkhaṇa-Sutta* (*Discourse on the Characteristic of Not-self*).[1] This theory is considered to be one of the cornerstones upon which the edifice of the Buddha's teachings is built. It is said to be a teaching specific to the Buddha.[2] Buddhism stands unique in the history of Indian thought in denying the existence of the self.[3]

Etymologically, the Pali word '*anattā*' consists of the negative prefix '*ana*' plus '*attā*' (Sanskrit, *ātman*), meaning not-self, non-ego, no-soul, or non-substantiality.[4] The term *anattā*, therefore, refers to a not-self or non-ego theory which rejects *attā* or self theories. Prior to and during the time of the Buddha there were many theories maintaining the existence of the self in some form or other. It is in contrast to them that the Buddha preached his new doctrine of not-self. In this context a brief account of these theories is a logical necessity for providing a background for understanding the doctrine of *anattā*.

## ANNIHILATIONISM AND ETERNALISM

As many as sixty-two views about the self were mentioned and refuted in the *Brahmajāla-Sutta*,[5] which is supposed to deal with every possible theory of the self. In the *Kathāvatthu*, the Buddha is said to have divided self views into two main groups: annihilationism (*ucchedavāda*) and eternalism (*sassatavāda*).[6] They represented the two extreme views which the Buddha tried to avoid while teaching the doctrine of the middle path.[7]

*Annihilationism* is the view that there exists in man an ego-entity as the principle of all physical and mental activities. But such a principle is only relatively permanent (lasting for a single lifetime), it does not survive after death. It is annihilated on the dissolution of the body. Since nothing continues to exist after death, rebirth is not possible in this view. Like Sartre, the nihilists think that after death life does not begin again, it is "a life in which one never recovers his stroke,"[8] to use Sartre's words. Ajita Kesakambala, a contemporary of the Buddha, was one of the outstanding nihilists. He maintained that there is no rebirth; a man consists of the four elements and when he dies, these elements return to their corresponding mass of great elements and he is completely annihilated.[9] Cārvāka, a materialist school of Indian philosophy, held a similar view.

> *"In this view, the four elements, earth, fire, water, air are the (only) categories. When these are changed into the form of a body, consciousness arises, like the power of intoxication when certain ingredients are mixed; when these elements are destroyed, consciousness ceases immediately. Thus the self (ātman) is only the body with the special characteristic of consciousness..."*[10]

In opposition to the annihilationist view, there is *eternalism.* The eternalists believe not only in the existence of an abiding ego-entity, but also in its immortality. Their view can be well described in these words: "This the world, this the self; after death I will become permanent, lasting, eternal, not liable to change. I will stand fast like unto the eternal."[11] The self is considered as something permanent (*nicca*), blissful (*sukha*) and not liable to change (*aviparināmadhamma*). The chief proponents of eternalism during the time of the Buddha were the Upaniṣadic thinkers. In fact, it is in the Upaniṣads that we find formulated a doctrine of the permanent self which has remained fundamental in Indian thought and it is this, more than anything else, which needs investigation when dealing with the Buddhist doctrine of *anattā.*

## ĀTMAN IN THE UPANIṢADS

The identity of *Brahman* and *ātman,* of the ultimate reality and the self, forms the fundamental thesis of the entire Upaniṣadic philosophy. The key subject of investigations in all the Upaniṣads can be expressed by the simple equation: *Brahman = ātman.*[12] What, then, is *ātman*? The word *ātman,* which is generally translated into English as self, is derived from *an* 'to breathe.' It is the breath of life.[13] Gradually its meaning is extended to cover life, soul or self. According Radhakrishnan, "*Ātman* is the principle of man's life, the soul that pervades his being, his breath, *prāṇa,* his intellect, *prajñā,* and transcends them. *Ātman* is what remains when everything that is not the self is eliminated."[14] The self, therefore, is a residue which is left after all physical and mental constituents of man's personality are analyzed. In the Chāndogya Upaniṣad, it is stated that the self transcends the bodily self of the materialists and also the self which experiences dreaming and dreamless sleep.[15] The ultimate state of the self cannot be known or explained, and can only be referred to as *Turīya.* And it is described in this way:

> "Turīya *is not that which is conscious of the internal world, nor*

> *that which is conscious of the external world, nor that which is conscious of both, nor is it a mass of consciousness. It is not consciousness, nor is it unconsciousness. It is unseen, undescribable, uncomprehensible, unknowable, unthinkable, and unnameable. It is the origin of the conscious self and that into which phenomena are again resolved. It is peace, bliss, and nonduality. This is* Turīya, *this is* ātman, *and this is to be realized."*[16]

Hence the self is independent of the body and on the dissolution of the body the self is not annihilated. "This body is mortal and all is subject to death. It is the abode of the self which is immortal and without body."[17] Moreover, the self is not the same as conscious experience; rather it is their 'origin.' The self 'lives' in mental acts, unifies and controls them.

> *"He who dwells in the mind, yet is within the mind, whom the mind does not know, whose body the mind is, who controls the mind from within, he is your self, the inner controller, the immortal."*[18]

The self is regarded as the subject of all experiences. It is the thinker of thoughts, the feeler of sensations and the doer of deeds. The question that we may raise now is: How does the self know itself? Can the self which is the subject of experiences be an experience? "What I must presuppose in order to know an object," says Kant, "I cannot know as an object."[19] But some Upaniṣadic thinkers differ from Kant when they think that the self is accessible in immediate experience in some sense or other. "Verily, the Self, Maitreyi, is to be seen, to be heard, to be reflected on, to be meditated upon; when, verily, the self is seen, heard, reflected on and known, then all this is known."[20] Śaṅkara, commenting on this passage, said that the self could be known through 'argument and reasoning' (*tarkenopapattayā*).

## THE SELF IS INDESCRIBABLE

Yājñavalkya, an Upaniṣadic thinker, does not accept the above-mentioned position. He thinks that the self cannot be known by any means of knowledge.[21] It is unknowable because in all knowledge the self is the knowing subject, and consequently can never be the object. He clearly says that "you cannot see the seer of seeing, you cannot hear the hearer of hearing, you cannot think the thinker of thinking, you cannot understand the understander of understanding. He is your self which is in all things."[22] As is mentioned earlier, the self is indescribable. One cannot point out what the self is like. Positive definition of the self is impossible. In talking about the self, we can only say that it is 'not anything'[23] that we find in experience. Hence Yājñavalkya says: "That self is not this, not this (*neti, neti*). He is incomprehensible for He cannot be comprehended."[24] Negative characters, however, should not mislead us into thinking that the self is non-being. The self has its own essence which we cannot describe. Its essential nature is said to be being (*sat*), consciousness (*cit*) and bliss (*ānanda*). These are different phrases for the same being.

> *"Self-being, self-consciousness, and self-delight are one. It is absolute being in which there is no nothingness. It is absolute consciousness in which there is no non-consciousness. It is absolute bliss in which there is no suffering or negation of bliss."*[25]

It should be noted here that the self, like the Sartrean consciousness or for-itself, is said to be '*neti*,' in the sense of not-being-this-object. The Platonic notion of 'otherness' may be applied here; the self is '*neti*' because it is a 'being-other-than-object.' But, unlike the for-itself which is non-being, the self is being, to use Hegel's phraseology, both in itself and for itself. It is being in itself because it does not depend on its objects for its existence; it is the ground of the phenomenal world. And it is being for itself because it is consciousness. Thus the self is the unity of being and consciousness. We may liken that self to the Sartrean being-in-itself-for-itself. For Sartre, the unity of being and consciousness as represented in the self always remains as man's unrealizable ideal. He says that such unity would exist only in God which is however a "non-entity" for Sartre.

We may add here that the Upaniṣadic thinkers are idealists. They think that the fullness of being is on the side of the knowing subject; the objects have no being-in-itself. For them, the objects "are not the *ātman*, the real 'self' of things, but mere *māyā*—that is to say, a sheer deceit, illusion."[26] In opposition to this stands Sartre's ontology described earlier. According to Sartre, the full positivity of being lies on the side of objects of consciousness, the so-called knowing subject is nothingness.

## YOGA OR MEDITATION

Yājñavalkya's contention that the self is unknowable represents opinions prevailing among the thinkers of the Early Upaniṣads. In the Middle and Later Upaniṣads we find a new position. There it is said that the self can be known, not by senses, reason or learning, but by intuitive insight. Thus the self which is hidden within all things and does not shine forth is said to be seen by the subtle seer with his superior awakened intuition.[27] Yoga is the method that enables the seer to develop his intuitive insight. "The self as the knowing subject can never become an object. It can be realized through Yoga."[28] One can see the self while in meditative rapture by the purification of knowledge: "By the peace of knowledge, one's nature is purified. In that way, however, by *meditation*, one does behold Him who is without parts."[29] Hence intuitive insight developed by practising meditation or *Yoga* is regarded by some Upaniṣadic thinkers as a means of knowing the self.

The intuition which sees the self is different from ordinary intuition which sees objects. The latter always presupposes the subject-object duality whereas the former does not. The seer's intuition is a kind of 'mystical insight'[30] by which the self knows itself without giving rise to the subject-object duality. According to Radhakrishnan, "Man has the faculty of divine insight or mystic intuition, by which he transcends the distinction of intellect and solves the riddles of reason."[31] In the mystic experience the self feels itself to be one with what it sees. This point has been explained by Plotinus:

*"In the vision of God, that which sees is not reason, but greater than and prior to reason, something presupposed by reason, as is the object of vision. He who then sees himself, when he sees, will see himself as a simple being, will be united to himself as such, will feel himself become such. We ought not even to say that he will see, but he will be that which he sees, if indeed it is possible any longer to distinguish seer and seen, and not boldly to affirm that the two are one. He belongs to God and is one with Him like two concentric circles; they are one when they coincide and two only when they are separated."*[32]

## BRAHMAN = ĀTMAN

To know the self, say the Upaniṣadic thinkers, is to know *Brahman*. This is because the self or *ātman* is identical with *Brahman*. *Brahman* is the ultimate principle as realized in the universe, *ātman* is the same principle as realized in man. The former stands for the transcendent unity, the latter for the immanent unity. In other words, *Brahman* is the substance of the world, *ātman* is the substance of the individual. And the two are one. *Brahman is ātman*.[33] "He who is there in the person and he who is yonder in the Sun—he is one."[34] This identity of the ultimate reality and the self is briefly expressed by the famous sayings "That art thou (*Tat tvam asi*)"[35] and "I am *Brahman* (*Aham Brahma asmi*)."[36] And in the compound word "unity of *Brahman* and *ātman*" is described the fundamental thesis of the Vedānta system.

Thus to know *ātman* amounts to the realization of *Brahman*. "In truth, he who knows the supreme *Brahman* becomes *Brahman* himself."[37] This is to say that the realization of *Brahman* is the attainment *Mokṣa* or liberation. Hence the knowledge of the self is called *Mokṣa*. This knowledge does not lead to liberation but is liberation itself:

*"For deliverance is not effected by the knowledge of the* ātman, *but it consists in this knowledge; it is not a consequence of the knowledge of the* ātman, *but this knowledge is itself already deliverance in all its fullness."*[38]

In reality, the true self of man is already and always *Brahman* and as such liberated, but its real nature is concealed by man's ignorance (*avidyā*). So long as man is ignorant he has to undergo a ceaseless series of transmigration. This sequence of rebirth comes to an end only when man knows his self to be *Brahman* and at once becomes liberated.

> *"Just as the flowing rivers disappear in the ocean casting off name and form, even so the* knower, *freed from name and form, attains the divine person, higher than the high.... He crosses over sorrow. He crosses over sins. Liberated from the knots of the secret place (of the heart), he becomes immortal."*[39]

Liberation is thus achieved not by a change of anything in the world, but by the disappearance of ignorance, a false outlook. That is, the change brought about here is only epistemic and not ontological.

## ĀTMAN AND THE TRANSCENDENTAL EGO

So far we have considered the doctrine of *ātman* in the Upaniṣads. This doctrine is rejected by the Buddhist. Before tracing his arguments against the self theory, we shall try to compare the Upaniṣadic conception of *ātman* rejected by the Buddhist with that of the transcendental ego repudiated by Sartre.

The transcendental ego is said to be the permanent subject of experiences; it transcends the body and the psychological states of the individual, it is what Husserl calls 'a transcendence in immanence.'[40] The transcendental ego always remains the same. It is the continuous background of changes in the stream of experience. The sense of personal identity and continuity has its source in the transcendental ego which functions as the unifying principle of consciousness. It 'lives' in consciousness and is viewed as its origin.

What has been said about the transcendental ego can, to some extent, truly be said about *ātman*. *Ātman*, we have seen, transcends the body and the empirical self. It is an eternal principle that generates, unifies and controls conscious experiences. *Ātman* also 'dwells' in consciousness. Like the transcendental ego in Husserl's sense, *ātman* remains as a 'residue' after the analysis of all physical and mental phenomena.

Another feature which makes the transcendental ego and *ātman* alike is that both of them are 'indescribable.'[41] They are empty of all determinations which are necessary for the possibility of positive definition. For the Upaniṣadic thinkers *ātman* is 'not this, not this,' and for Husserl, the transcendental ego is 'pure ego and *nothing* further.'[42]

Furthermore, the transcendental ego is the 'Absolute Being'[43] in the sense of being the ground of all meaning. Hence all being is given as related to a single core, i.e., the transcendental ego. The phenomenal world derives its meaning as existing reality from the ego.[44] Viewed in this way, the transcendental ego leads Husserl to admit that his philosophy is 'transcendental-phenomenological idealism.'[45] The idealistic trend, however, is more obvious in the case of *ātman*. The Upaniṣadic thinkers regard *ātman* as 'absolute being,'[46] and the phenomenal world as *māyā* or illusion. The world has no being in itself; its appearance is effected by ignorance (*avidyā*) of the knowing subject.

The transcendental ego as the subject of experience can never be known as an object. The ego, however, has an immediate knowledge of itself after phenomenological reduction is performed. This reduction is the 'necessary operation' which enables the ego to know itself. *Ātman*, like the ego, is not included in what is given to our experience for it is its subject. *Ātman* knows itself by the performance of *Yoga*. Thus *Yoga* is the necessary method that makes self-knowledge possible. Like phenomenological reduction which suspends the natural attitude, *Yoga* eliminates all kinds of hindrances so that the mind is in a position to grasp the object in its primordiality.[47] In the highest stage of concentration (*samādhi*), the mind becomes one with its object and therefore attains the mystic state. And it is in this state that the self knows itself.

So far we have attempted to show certain resemblances between the transcendental ego and *ātman*. Nevertheless, we do not mean to say that the two are exactly the same. There are two essential characteristics of *ātman* which the transcendental ego seems to lack: immortality and identity with the ultimate reality. Husserl nowhere claims that the ego can be identified with the ultimate reality. Nor does he assert that the ego is immortal. Koestenbaum remarks:

> *"The conception of both the death and the birth (i.e., the non-existence) of the Transcendental Ego is impossible. It requires the Transcendental Ego to think, imagine, or conceive the death and birth of an ego... Birth and death are properties of objects and apply only to the empirical ego."*[48]

These statements only imply that the transcendental ego must necessarily be permanent in order that the moments of arising and ceasing of mental acts can be observed. From this it does not follow that the transcendental ego can survive after death. If the ego were immortal, its immortality would not be proved by phenomenological reduction. So it is still doubtful whether the transcendental ego is immortal or not. Kant says that as far as the immortality of the soul is concerned, he has no theoretical proof of it; yet he has to 'postulate' the immortality in order to make morality possible. This kind of postulate is avoided by Husserl who wants to do a presuppositionless philosophy.

The conclusion that we can draw from the foregoing comparisons is that *ātman* in the Upaniṣads is something like what Husserl's transcendental ego would be if it were endowed with immortality and identity with the ultimate reality. The Upaniṣadic thinkers assume that *ātman* is immortal and identical with *Brahman* because they want to justify their quest for *Mokṣa* or liberation. Their religious life would be meaningless without the postulate of immortality of the self.

## THE BUDDHA'S REJECTION OF THE PERMANENT EGO

All kinds of permanent self—be they called *ātman* or transcendental ego—are rejected by the Buddhist:

> *"Whatever be the theories about the* ātman *held by the various thinkers during the time of the Buddha and thereafter, the Buddhist doctrine of* anattā, *as preserved in the* Theravāda *tradition, contradicts them all in all-embracing sweep."*[49]

We shall now turn to consider the Buddhist's arguments against the self theory.

The conception of the permanent self or *ātman* described above was known to Buddhism.[50] By the self the Buddhist understands that permanent, substantial ego-entity which is the principle of thoughts and actions. In brief, the self is viewed as the subject of experience:

> *"Whatever is the self for me that speaks, that experiences and knows, that experiences now here, now there, the function of deeds that are lovely and that are depraved, it is this self for me that is permanent, stable, eternal, not subject to change, that will stand firm like unto the eternal."*[51]

The self is said to possess bliss and autonomy. These notions of the self are not acceptable to the Buddhist. The Buddha flatly denies that there exists in man an ego-entity which is permanent, blissful and autonomous. His arguments against the self are analytical because they are based on the analysis of the personality.

## FIVE AGGREGATES

The person (*puggala*), when analyzed, is found to consist of five aggregates (Pali, *Khandha* = Sanskrit, *Skandha*). These aggregates neither singly nor collectively constitute any permanent self, nor is there to be found a self apart from them. The five aggregates are those of corporeality (*rūpa*), feeling (*vedanā*), perception (*saññā*), mental formations (*saṅkhāra*) and consciousness (*viññāṇa*).[52] The following is a brief description of these aggregates:

1. The aggregate of *corporeality* comprises the material con-

stituents of the individual. The body belongs to this aggregate. In the aggregate of corporeality are included the traditional Four Primary Elements (*mahābhūta-rūpa* ), namely, solidity, fluidity, heat and motion, and also the Derivatives of the Four Primary Elements (*upādāya-rūpa* ).[53] In the Derivatives are included our five material sense-organs, i.e., eye, ear, nose, tongue and body, and their corresponding objects in the external world., i.e., visible form, sound, odor, taste, and tangible things, and also some physical components of the body. Thus the whole realm of matter, both internal and external, is included in the aggregate of corporeality.

2. The aggregate of *feeling* as one of the four nonmaterial groups is the affective aspect of mental activities. It has the characteristic of enjoying the "taste" of an object.[54] The Commentary of the Dhammasaṅganī describes the nature of feeling with a metaphor:

> *"As regards enjoying the taste of an object, the remaining associated states enjoy it only partially. Of contact there is (the function of) mere touching, of perception the mere noting or perceiving, of volition the mere coordinating (the associated states of exerting or being active), of consciousness the mere cognizing. But feeling alone, through governance, proficiency, mastery, enjoys the taste of an object. For feeling is like the king, the remaining states are like the cook."*[55]

There are three kinds of feeling: pleasant, painful and neutral.[56]

3. The aggregate of *perception* is the cognitive dimension of experience. Its function is to recognize objects, physical or mental.[57] In the Mahāvedalla-Sutta it is explained as a relatively simple form of cognition which consists in the discernment, recognition and assimilation of sensations.[58] According to Mrs. Rhys Davids, perception means that sense-perception which discerns, recognizes and gives class-reference to the impressions of sense.[59] There are six classes of perception: perception of visible forms, sounds, odors, tastes, tangible things, and of mental objects.[60]

4. The aggregate of *mental formations* is a collective term for numerous conative aspects of mental activity which, in addition to feeling and perception, are present in a single moment of consciousness. In the *Abhidhamma,* fifty mental formations are mentioned.

5. The aggregate of *consciousness* is defined by Buddhaghosa as "everything taken together that has the characteristic of cognizing."[61] Consciousness is a simple awareness of the presence of an object. It does not recognize the object; that is a function of perception.

> *"When the eye comes in contact with a color, for instance blue, visual consciousness arises which simply is awareness of the presence of a color; but it does not recognize that it is blue. There is no recognition at this stage. It is perception ... that recognizes that it is blue."*[62]

Hence some scholars render *viññāṇa* as 'cognition' and *saññā* as 'recognition.' There are six kinds of consciousness, in relation to six internal faculties and corresponding six external objects.[63]

These aggregates are a fivefold classification in which the Buddha summed up all the physical and mental phenomena of existence, and in particular those which appear to the ignorant man as his self or ego. Of the five aggregates, only the first group refers to material constituents, the remaining aggregates are groupings of mental phenomena. It is worth noting that the Buddhist analysis of mind (*citta*) into feeling, perception, mental formations and consciousness is very similar to the tripartite division of mind into affection, conation and cognition so common in Western psychology. By comparison, we find that feeling (*vedanā*) refers to the category of affection, mental formations (*saṅkhāra*) to conation, and perception (*saññā*) and consciousness (*viññāṇa*) to cognition.[64] The tripartite division of mind, however, is viewed by some Western psychologists as an artificial and oversimplified analysis. But, as Flügel says, some such classification is probably necessary if we are to obtain any kind of ordered understanding of the rich facts of mental experience.[65]

It should be emphasized here that the five aggregates merely form an abstract classification, none of them has real existence. For example, the aggregate of mental formations which comprises fifty mental factors becomes an empty abstraction if it is considered apart from its constituent parts. Each aggregate cannot exist in complete isolation from the others. They are mutually dependent and therefore inseparable. In the *Abhidhamma,* the aggregates of feeling, perception and mental formations are called '*cetasika,*' meaning 'that which is associated with consciousness.'[66] These three aggregates form different aspects and properties of consciousness; they naturally arise and perish together with consciousness. "They are to consciousness what redness, softness, sweetness, etc., are to an apple and have as little separate existence as those qualities."[67] This clearly indicates that consciousness for the Buddhist has inner 'contents' or 'properties.' As Sāriputta says:

> *"That which is feeling, your reverence, that which is perception and that which is consciousness—these states are associated, not dissociated, and it is not possible to lay down a difference between these states, having analyzed them again and again. Your reverence, whatever one feels, that one perceives; whatever one perceives, of that one is conscious."*[68]

## ARGUMENTS AGAINST THE SELF

The Buddha's arguments for the denial of the self are based on this *pañcakkhandha* analysis. In the *Anattalakkhaṇa-Sutta* the Buddha begins his argument with an attack on what may be called the 'autonomous self.' The autonomy of the self is propounded by the Upaniṣadic thinkers who say that the self is the 'inner controller' of mind and body.[69] The Buddha denies that there is such a controller of the five aggregates. Since there is no mastery over them, one can very well say that they have no owner or controller. The Buddha says:

> *"Body, monks, is not self. Now were this body self, monks, this*

*body would not tend to sickness, and one might say in regard to the body: 'Let body become thus for me, let body not become thus for me.' And it is because body is not-self that body tends to sickness and one cannot say of it, 'let body become thus for me, let body not become thus for me.'"*[70]

The same argument is repeated for the remaining aggregates, namely feeling, perception, mental formations, and consciousness. Buddhaghosa, therefore, concludes: "the mode of unruliness is the characteristic of not-self."[71]

The Buddha then criticizes the view that there exists in man a permanent and blissful self. He says that the person, when analyzed, is found to consist of five aggregates and nothing else. And the aggregates are impermanent and subject to suffering. The Buddha then asks the monks: "Is it proper to look upon that which is impermanent, subject to suffering and liable to change as, 'this is mine, this I am, this is my self?" The monks reply, "It is not."[72] Thus the five aggregates are not-self because they lack the permanence and bliss which are regarded as the essential characteristics of the self.

When the Buddha says that the five aggregates are not self, he does not mean to imply that there exists a self which transcends these aggregates. According to the Buddha, the transcendental self does not exist because it cannot be found either inside or outside the five aggregates. That is why the Buddha asks:

*"If self, monks, and what belongs to self are not truly and really found* (anupalabbhamāne)*, is it not, monks, a perfectly foolish doctrine to hold the point of view, 'This the world, this the self; after death I will become permanent, lasting, eternal, not liable to change, I will stand fast like unto the eternal?"*[73]

## THE BUDDHA AND HUME

Here we find that the Buddha's attitude towards the problem of the self is different from that of the Upaniṣadic thinkers. In the

*Chāndogya Upaniṣad,* Prajāpati, assuming the existence of the self, tries to locate it within the personality. Failing to identify it with any of the constituents of the personality, he continues to assume that it must exist within the personality and is not satisfied with the results of the purely empirical investigation.[74] The Buddha, on the contrary, assumes neither the existence or nonexistence of the self, and when the empirical investigation fails to reveal it, concludes that no such self exists because there is no evidence for its existence. In this respect the Buddha's attitude is similar to Hume's. In rejecting the Cartesian view of the self, Hume maintains that the self does not exist because it cannot be truly discovered. He says that on reflecting upon himself, he discovers only the stream of changing perceptions; no self is found.

> *"For my part, when I enter most intimately into what I call myself I always stumble on some particular perception or other, of heat or cold, light or shade, love or hatred, pain or pleasure. I never can catch myself at any time without a perception, and never can observe anything but the perception."*[75]

Hume then asserts that it is the composition of these perceptions which forms the self.

> *"I may venture to affirm of the rest of mankind, that they are nothing but* a bundle or collection of different perceptions, *which succeed each other with an inconceivable rapidity, and are in a perpetual flux and movement."*[76]

The Buddha, like Hume, reflects upon himself and finds nothing but the changing aggregates of corporeality, feeling, perception, mental formations and consciousness. He then concludes that the so-called person (*puggala*) is a mere collection of the five aggregates. Thus it is said: "Just as it is on condition of various parts that the word chariot is used, just so is it that when the aggregates are there we talk of a 'living-being' (*satta*)."[77] This has been explained by Buddhaghosa in the Visuddhimagga:

*"Therefore just as when various parts, such as axle, wheel, frame and pole, are put together in a certain manner, the word 'chariot' comes into use, but when each of the parts is examined no chariot in the ultimate sense can be found ... so on condition of the five clung-to aggregates the word 'being' or 'person' comes into use, but when each of the aggregates is examined no such being can be found. It is a misconception that makes one say 'I am' or 'I.' In the ultimate sense there are only name-and-form."*[78]

## THREE CHARACTERISTICS

In retrospect, we find that the Buddhist doctrine of *anattā* is a necessary corollary to the teaching of *anicca* (impermanence). The five aggregates are not-self because they are found to be impermanent. The Buddha says:

*"The five aggregates, monks, are impermanent; whatever is impermanent, that is subject to suffering; whatever is subject to suffering, that is not-self; whatever is not-self, that is not mine, that I am not, that is not my self."*[79]

Buddhaghosa explains that the five aggregates are "*impermanent* because of non-eternality and having a beginning and end; *subject to suffering* because of being oppressed by growth and decay and through being a cause of suffering, ... *empty* because of the absence of an owner, a tenant, a doer, or a feeler or a superintendent; and *not-self* because themselves without owner, etc."[80] This is an interpretation of the Three Characteristics (*tilakkhaṇa*), which are stated in this formula:

"All component things are impermanent.
All component things are suffering.
All *dhammas* are not-self."[81]

Here it should be noted that in the first two sentences the word *saṅkhārā* (component things) is used, but in its place in the third sentence the word *dhamma* is used. Why wasn't the word *saṅkhārā* used in the last sentence? Here lies the crux of the whole matter.

The term *saṅkhārā* denotes conditioned things like the five aggregates. If the third sentence said "All component things are not self," then it would imply that although component things are not self, there may be a self outside component things, transcending the five aggregates. In order to avoid misunderstanding, the term *dhamma* is used in the third sentence. This term is much wider in scope than *saṅkhārā*. It includes not only conditioned things but also the non-conditioned (*asaṅkhata dhamma*), i.e. *Nirvāṇa* (Pali, *Nibbāna*). There is nothing in the universe or outside which is not included in the term *dhamma*. Hence the statement, "All *dhammas* are not-self," means that there is no self or substance, not only in the five aggregates, but also everywhere outside them or apart from them. This clearly shows that early Buddhism teaches the selflessness of the person and of *dhammas*. Mahāyāna Buddhism maintains exactly the same position on this point when it puts emphasis on both selflessness of the person (*pudgala-nairātmya*) and selflessness of the *dhamma* (*dharma-nairātmya*).

## DEPENDENT ORIGINATION

Thus the doctrine of not-self denies not only the self within the personality but also the substance of the phenomenal world. It is opposed to the Upaniṣadic view that *ātman* is the substance of the person and *Brahman* is the substance of the universe. In brief, it rejects the substance view of the world. For the Buddhist, everything is empty of self-reality. Nothing exists in itself, for each existence is conditioned by causes outside itself. Since all phenomena have nothing substantial or perdurable in them, they are in a condition not of static being, but of perpetual becoming (*bhava*). Rhys Davids says: "According to the Buddhist, there is no Being, there is only a Becoming."[82] The phenomenal world, therefore, is in a state of continuous flux or flow. All things, without exception, are nothing but chains of momentary events, instantaneous 'bits' of existence. In short, they are momentary (*khaṇika*). In the Buddhist view not only are eternal entities such as God, self, or matter, denied reality, but even the simple stability of empirical objects is regarded as imaginary. We can easily see that the Upaniṣadic notion of being (*sat*) and the Sartrean conception of being-in-itself (*l'être-en-soi*) are not acceptable to the Buddhist. A belief either in absolute being or in absolute nothingness is considered to be an extreme view. The Buddha says:

> "*Everything* is; *this, Kaccāna, is one extreme view. Everything* is not; *this the second extreme view. Avoiding both these extremes, the* Tathāgata *teaches a doctrine by the middle path.*"[83]

The doctrine of the middle path is generally known as Dependent Origination (*paṭiccasamuppāda*). According to the Buddha, all phenomena are subject to the laws of causation. There is nothing haphazard or predetermined. Every element, though appearing only for a single moment, is a dependently-originating element because it depends for its arising on what has gone before it. That is the meaning of Dependent Origination. The law of causation can be expressed by the following formula:

> "When this is, that is (*Imasmiṁ sati idaṁ hoti*);
> This arising, that arises (*Imassuppādā idaṁ uppajjati*);
> When this is not, that is not (*Imasmiṁ asati idaṁ na hoti*);
> This ceasing, that ceases (*Imassa nirodha idaṁ nirujjhati*)."[84]

This abstract formula shows the logic of the causal law without contents.[85] The general principle of Dependent Origination is described by a series of twelve factors:

1. Conditioned by ignorance (*avijjā*) are karma-formations (*saṅkhārā*).
2. Conditioned by karma-formations is consciousness (*viññāṇa*).
3. Conditioned by consciousness is name-and-form (*nāma-rūpa*).
4. Conditioned by name-and-form are the six faculties (*saḷāyatana*).
5. Conditioned by the six faculties is contact (*phassa*).

6. Conditioned by contact is feeling (*vedanā*).
7. Conditioned by feeling is desire (*taṇhā*).
8. Conditioned by desire is grasping (*upādāna*).
9. Conditioned by grasping is becoming (*bhava*).
10. Conditioned by becoming is birth (*jāti*).
11. Conditioned by birth are old age, death, grief, sorrow, suffering, lamentation and despair (*jarāmaraṇasoka ...*)

This is how life arises, exists and continues. If we put this formula in its reverse order, we come to the cessation of the process:

Through the cessation of ignorance, karma-formations cease; through the cessation of karma-formations, consciousness ceases ... through the cessation of birth, old age, death, grief, sorrow, suffering, lamentation and despair cease.[86]

It should be emphasized here that each of these Factors is both conditioned (*paṭiccasamuppanna*) and conditioning (*paṭiccasamuppāda*).[87] Hence they are all relative and interdependent; nothing is absolute or exists as independent substance. Thus no first cause is accepted. Ignorance (*avijjā*) should not be viewed as the first cause of the whole process because ignorance itself is conditioned by the cankers (*āsava*). "From the uprising of the cankers is the uprising of the ignorance, from the stopping of the cankers is the stopping of ignorance."[88]

The law of causality in early Buddhism is not subjective. Nor is it a category imposed by the mind on phenomena. Its objectivity is emphasized. "Dependent Origination is said to have the characteristics of objectivity, necessity, invariability and conditionality."[89] That a causal sequence occurs independently of us and that all we do is to discover this, is implied in the following description of Dependent Origination:

> *"What is Dependent Origination? Conditioned by birth are old age and death. Whether the* Tathāgata *arises or not, this order exists, namely, the fixed nature of phenomena, the regular pattern of phenomena or conditionality. This the* Tathāgata *discovers and comprehends ..."*[90]

The doctrine of Dependent Origination and the analysis of the five aggregates give support to the *anattā* doctrine. The person is analyzed into five constituent parts and these parts are combined to constitute the personality, not by a unifying ego-principle, but by the causal law. The self is not required for effecting the synthesis of the five aggregates. It is the law of Dependent Origination that unifies them.

Moreover, the law of Dependent Origination determines that the five aggregates are dependently originated (*paṭiccasamuppanna*). No aggregate arises without causes. The Buddha says:

> *"And also the causes and conditions of the arising of these aggregates are impermanent, painful and not-self. How could that which has arisen through something impermanent, painful and not-self as its root, be itself permanent, blissful and a self?"*[91]

The Buddha denies that there exists a permanent self in the collection of these impersonal aggregates. In place of the Upaniṣadic teaching, "Let no man try to find what speech is, let him know the speaker; let him not try to find what the seen-thing is, let him know the seer; not what the doing is, but the doer, etc.," the Buddha teaches that there is no doer, only doing exists; no seer, only seeing, etc. As Buddhaghosa writes: "In all becomings, places of birth, durations and abodes there appears just the name-and-form proceeding by way of cause and effect. Beyond the cause he sees not a doer, beyond the proceeding of results he sees not anyone to enjoy the results."[92] To show the impersonality and utter emptiness of existence, Buddhaghosa quotes the following verse:

"Mere suffering exists, no sufferer.  
The deed is, but no doer.  
*Nirvāṇa* is, but not he who enters it.  
The path is, but no traveller."[93]

The Upaniṣadic thinkers, as we saw, agree with the Buddhist in admitting that all phenomena are impermanent and liable to change. The Upaniṣadic thinkers, however, believe that beneath changing phenomena lies an eternal entity identified as *Brahman,* and that behind the stream of discrete experiences exists an abiding principle called *ātman*. The Buddhist, on the contrary, contends that all phenomena are in a state of flux and nothing is behind them. There is no thinker behind the thought. As William James says, "the thought is itself the thinker."[94] If the thought is removed, there is no thinker to be found. Here the Buddhist view is diametrically opposed to the Cartesian *cogito ergo sum: "I think, therefore I am."* It is rather close to Sartre's view, according to which there is no thinker apart from the object thought.[95]

By denying the existence of the self, the Buddha is said to have avoided two extreme views, namely, eternalism and annihilationism. These views are related to the self theory. Those who believe that the self exists have to admit that it is perishable or imperishable. If they admit that the self is perishable, then they are annihilationists. If they admit that the self is imperishable, then they are eternalists. The Buddha regards the two extremes as 'wrong views' (*micchādiṭṭhi*). "Both these extremes, monks, have been avoided by the *Tathāgata,* and it is a middle doctrine he teaches."[96]

## ANATTĀ AND NIRVĀṆA

The Buddhist doctrine of *anattā* has a practical bearing since it "has moral perfection as its purpose."[97] Just as the Upaniṣadic conception of *Mokṣa* cannot be justified without assuming the existence of *ātman,* so also the Buddhist conception of Nirvana cannot be accounted for without admitting the *anattā* doctrine. Nyanatiloka writes:

> *"Without understanding the egolessness of existence, it is not possible to gain a real understanding of the Buddha-word; and it is not possible without it to realize that goal of emancipation and deliverance of mind proclaimed by the Buddha. This doctrine of egolessness of existence forms the essence of the Buddha's doctrine of emancipation."*[98]

If the self existed, then the religious life proclaimed by the Buddha would have become useless for the cessation of suffering. The Buddha once took up a little pellet of cow dung, and said to a monk:

> *"If the getting of a selfhood* (attabhāva) *so small as this, monk, permanent, stable, eternal, by nature unchanging, was possible, then the living of the holy life for the best destruction of suffering would not be set forth. But inasmuch, monk, as there is no getting of a selfhood even so small as this, unchanging ... therefore the living of the holy life for the best destruction of suffering is set forth."*[99]

According to the Buddha, the idea of the self is a wrong view because it has no corresponding reality. What is worse is that the idea itself generates suffering. Hence the Buddha says "I do not see, monks, that grasping of the theory of self, from the grasping of which there would not arise grief, suffering, anguish, lamentation, despair."[100] Also, "in brief, the five aggregates of grasping are suffering."[101] That is the crux of the Buddhist attitude towards the theory of self. The self is considered as the manifestation of the subtlest form of grasping called *attavādupādāna*.[102] This grasping of the self is the main origin of suffering. It is similar to 'self-love' which some Western psychologists believe to be the centre of all desires and actions.[103] This self-love, according to William James, is the cause of selfishness. "A man in whom self-seeking of any sort is largely developed is said to be selfish."[104] It manifests itself as the sense of 'I' and 'Mine' (*Ahaṅkāramaṅkāra*). We may liken the grasping of the self to 'narcissism' in Freudian psychoanalysis. The similarity between them is implied in the words of Erich Fromm: "It is the goal of man to overcome one's narcissism. Perhaps this principle is nowhere expressed more radically than in Buddhism."[105]

Thus the main purpose of the Buddha's teaching of *anattā* is to enable his disciples to shed the grasping of the self theory. To attain *Nirvāṇa,* one has to get rid of the personality belief (*sakkāyadiṭṭhi*) and the conceit of 'I am' (*asmimāna*). So long as grasping of the self in any form persists, there can be no real emancipation. In the *Mūlapariyāya-Sutta,* the Buddha emphasizes the need for absolute abandonment of the conceit of 'I am' in all things including *Nirvāṇa.*[106] And it is on account of grasping of the five aggregates that the conceit of 'I am' arises.

> *"It is by grasping that the conceit of 'I am' arises and not without grasping. By grasping of what? It is by grasping of corporeality ... feeling ... perception ... mental formations ... consciousness that the conceit of 'I am' arises, and not without grasping."*[107]

The conceit of 'I am' is considered so detrimental to the religious quest that it is singled out as one which must be eliminated. With regard to the question, "which one thing is to be got rid of", it is said that "the conceit of 'I am' is the one thing which is to be got rid of."[108] It is by eliminating the conceit of 'I am' in the five aggregates that one attains liberation. The Buddha says:

> *"Whatever corporeality, Kappa, be it past, present or future ... you behold thus: 'This is not mine, this I am not, this is not my self.' So knowing things objectively as they are by perfect insight, one, having forsaken grasping, is free. (Similarly with regard to the other four aggregates). Thus knowing, thus seeing, Kappa ... the mind has gone away from all sense of 'I' and 'Mine',* (ahaṅkāramamaṅkāra) *gone away from egotism* (māna)*, gone away from all distinctions, calmed and wholly released."*[109]

## WISE AND UNWISE ATTENTION

It is made quite clear by the Buddha that the idea of the self is possible only in and through the five aggregates. "Of those ascetics or *Brahmins* who variously conceive of the self, all of them conceive either one or all of the five aggregates of grasping (as the self)."[110] It is by unwise attention that one sees the self in the impersonal aggregates. In Buddhism there are two kinds of attention: wise attention (*yoniso-manasikāra*) and unwise attention (*ayoniso-manasikāra*).[111] One sees the true nature of things by wise attention, not by unwise attention. Wise attention limits itself to what is really given whereas unwise attention asserts more than it knows. Unwise attention therefore introduces a self into the selfless aggregates; that is, it turns the mind against the truth so that one sees "the self in what is not-self."[112] Unwise attention gives rise to distortions (*vipallāsa*) of perception, thought and view. A man of unwise attention perceives, thinks and views permanence in what is essentially impermanent, bliss in what subject to suffering, self in what is not-self, and delight in what is essentially repulsive and disgusting.[113] In other words, he fails to see things as they really are (*yathābhūtaṁ*). Thus the idea of the self is a false idea caused by unwise attention. The selflessness of things is difficult to detect because it is hidden by compactness.

> *"The characteristic of not-self does not become apparent because, when resolution into the various elements is not given attention, it is hidden by compactness ... When the resolution of the compact (*ghana-vinibbhoga*) is effected by resolving it into its elements, the characteristic of not-self becomes apparent in its true nature."*[114]

## THREE KINDS OF DESIRE

Sartre, as we have seen, maintains that the self is constituted by impure reflection.[115] In this respect, his position is similar to the Buddha's. The Buddha, like Sartre, thinks that the self is constituted by unwise attention and becomes one of fifty mental formations of the fourth aggregate.[116] Thus the Sartrean impure reflection and the Buddhist unwise attention appear to be more or less alike. The difference between them, however, lies in the fact that whereas impure reflection is reflection in bad faith and creates the self in order to hide from its freedom, unwise attention is attention influenced by desire (*taṇhā*) and creates the self in order to satisfy the desire. The impact of desires on man's view is recognized in Buddhism. Therefore, it is said: "Conditioned by desire is grasping."[117] From this it follows that the grasping of the self is caused and conditioned by desire. That is why the Buddha says: "The five aggregates of grasping are rooted in desire."[118] There are three kinds of desire, namely, desire for sensuous pleasure (*kāmataṇhā*), desire for existence (*bhavataṇhā*) and desire for annihilation (*vibhavataṇhā*).[119] It is interesting to note that the Buddhist threefold division of desires is comparable to Freud's conceptions of libido, ego instinct and death instinct.[120] Sartre has also described the nature of desires, and concluded that all of them are reducible to either the desire to be or the desire to have,[121] which, in our opinion, is equivalent to the desire for existence in Buddhism.

The desire for existence (*bhavataṇhā*) is man's craving for self-preservation. It drives him to search for something in himself that can survive after death. The belief in the immortal self (*sassata-diṭṭhi*) is influenced by this desire. The desire for annihilation (*vibhavataṇhā*), on the other hand, is the craving for self-extinction. The belief in self annihilation (*uccheda-diṭṭhi*) is rooted in this desire. It manifests itself in the form of self-disgust and despair. The nihilist seeks for the extinction of this life because he believes that "as soon as this self is annihilated on the dissolution of the body, after death, that is peace, that is the supreme goal, that is reality."[122]

## THE BUDDHA AS AN EXPERIENTIALIST

In the preceding discussion we have considered the various arguments which form the denial of the self. The Buddha's arguments, as we mentioned earlier, are analytical for the reason that they consist in the analysis of the person into the five aggregates. Nevertheless, the Buddhist analysis is not a logical one; rather it is a phenomenological analysis in the sense that it analyzes and describes what is given to our experience. In Rahula's words, "it is an analytical method based on mindfulness, awareness, vigilance, observation."[123] The Buddha is not a rationalist; he is an experientialist or empiricist.[124] In the *Saṅgārava-Sutta* the Buddha classifies his predecessors and contemporaries into three groups:

(I) The traditionalists (*anussavika*), who derive their knowledge wholly from a scriptural tradition and interpretations based on it;

(2) The rationalists and metaphysicians (*takkī, vīmaṁsī*), who derive their knowledge from reasoning and speculation, and

(3) The experientialists, who depend on personal experience of higher knowledge.

The Buddha then says that he belongs to the third group.[125] According to him, an appeal to experience is necessary for judging the truth of a theory. The teaching of the Buddha is qualified as *ehipassika,* inviting one to 'come and see,' because it can be tested by experience. Experience here is not a mere sense experience but also intuition and insight. The Buddha does not regard scriptural tradition and reasoning based on logic as sufficient criteria of knowledge. "The weight of tradition, the use of logic and reason have their limits and an appeal to experience is necessary."[126]

## TWO FORMS OF MEDITATION

Thus the characteristic of not-self can be seen by intuitive insight. "What is not-self, that is not mine, that I am not, that is not myself. Thus should it be *seen* by perfect wisdom as it really is."[127] In order to develop insight which sees the true nature of things, one has to practise the Buddhist method called meditation. This practice aims at *'knowing and seeing things as they are (yathābhūtañāṇadassana).'* It reminds us of Husserl's slogan: *'back to the things themselves.'*

The word meditation is a poor substitute for the original term *bhāvanā* which means 'mental development.'[128] The Buddhist *bhāvanā* aims at cleansing the mind of all prejudices and distractions, and cultivating such qualities as concentration, awareness and mindfulness, leading finally to the attainment of perfect wisdom which sees things as they really are (*yathābhūtaṁ*). There are two forms of meditation: development of concentration (*samatha* or *samādhi*) and development of insight (*vipassanā*).

Concentration (*samādhi*) is the unwavering state of mind in which attention is fixed on a single object. Buddhaghosa writes: "Therefore that state, by the strength of which mind and mental properties are placed on one object fittingly and well, without wavering, without scattering, should be known as concentration."[129] In the state of concentration, the mind is freed from five hindrances (*nivaraṇa*), namely, sensuous desire (*kāmachanda*), ill-will (*vyāpāda*), sloth and torpor (*thīna-middha* ), restlessness and anxiety (*uddhacca-kukkucca*) and doubt (*vicikicchā*). The elimination of the hindrances sets the mind in concentration and this in turn makes it possible for it to have knowledge and insight of things as they are. This is to say that concentration is a preparatory stage for the other form of meditation, i.e., *vipassanā* or insight. That is why it is said that "concentration is the cause of knowing and seeing things as they are."[130] Hence concentration is not the final goal of meditation. It is a path leading to *vipassanā,* insight into the true nature of things. *Vipassanā* or insight meditation is a phenomenological investigation of physical and mental phenomena; it is a reflection (*anupassanā*) upon body, feelings, consciousness and other psychic factors.[131] *Vipassanā* meditation, however, is not the same as the method of pure phenomenology because it does not bracket the existence of the world; rather it aims at discovering the 'instantaneous being' of things in the world. That is why the final outcome of the Buddhist's *vipassanā* meditation is different from that of Husserl's phenomenological reduction. While the reduction reveals the essences of things and the transcendental ego of the person, *vipassanā* meditation discloses the non-substantiality of things and the egolessness of the person.

According to the Buddha, impermanence, suffering and selflessness are the true nature or common characteristics (*sāmañña-lakkhaṇa*) of component things; therefore, things have no essence (*sāra*). By means of *vipassanā* meditation, one sees these three characteristics of things and, thus eliminates distortions (*vipallāsa*) caused by unwise attention (*ayoniso-manasikāra*). The insight into the true nature of things gives rise to non-grasping and enables one to attain emancipation, *Nirvāṇa*:

*"A person who knows and sees the thing as it is does not need to make an effort of will to feel disinterested and renounce. It is in the nature of things* (dhammatā) *that a person who knows and sees as it really is feels disinterested and renounces. One who has felt disinterested and has renounced does not need an effort of will to realize the knowledge and insight of emancipation. It is in the nature of things that one who has felt disinterested and renounced realizes the knowledge and insight of emancipation."*[132]

Thus Buddhist meditation has *Nirvāṇa* or the complete cessation of suffering as its ultimate goal. Husserl's phenomenological reduction serves a different purpose since it is proposed as a 'logical-epistemological device'[133] for establishing philosophy as a rigorous science.

## VIPASSANĀ: THE BUDDHIST MEDITATION

*Vipassanā-bhāvanā* or insight meditation is claimed to be a specifically Buddhist method; concentration meditation (*samatha bhāvanā*) forms part of almost all Indian religious practice. In the Upaniṣadic literatures, concentration meditation is known as *Yoga*. As mentioned earlier, the Upaniṣadic thinkers regard *Yoga* as a method which enables them to realize *ātman*.[134] Concentration consists of different degrees, the highest of which is a mystic state, within which a mystic intuition of *ātman* takes place. The Buddha, before his Enlightenment, studied *Yoga* under different teachers and attained the highest mystic state; but he was not satisfied with it because it did not give complete emancipation. In the mystic states such as 'the Sphere of Nothingness' or 'the Sphere of Neither-Perception Nor-Non-Perception,' there is only emptiness; no *ātman* is found. Here is the point where the Buddha departs from the Upaniṣadic thinkers: while the latter consider *Yoga* as the method for developing insight which realizes *ātman*, the former considers it as the method that enables one to find only emptiness. For the Buddha, *Yoga* does not lead us to the attainment of complete emancipation as the Upaniṣadic thinkers claim. He considered the mystic state of Yoga only as 'happy living in this existence' or 'peaceful living' (*santavihāra*) and nothing more.[135] The Buddha later discovered a method that enabled him to attain the complete cessation of suffering. He called it *vipassanā* or insight meditation. It is a method unique to Buddhism. For practising *vipassanā* meditation, a certain degree of concentration is required. Concentration has two degrees of development: (I) 'Neighborhood concentration' (*upacāra-samādhi*), which approaches the first 'trance' (*jhāna*) without attaining it; (2) 'Attainment concentration' (*appanā-samādhi*), which is the concentration present in the four 'trances' (*jhāna*). These 'trances' are mental states beyond the reach of the fivefold sense-activity; no visual or audible impressions arise at such time, no bodily feeling is felt. In 'trances' the mind is so absorbed in its object that it cannot reflect upon concrete psychic factors like feelings, emotions, etc., thus the concentration necessary for arising of insight is in the level of Neighborhood concentration. This insight "is attainable only during Neighborhood concentration, not during Attainment concentration."[136] This means that Neighborhood concentration leads to *vipassanā* or insight while Attainment concentration leads to the mystic states of *Yoga*. This shows how *vipassanā* meditation, as a method, differs from *Yoga*. The former is based on the empirical, concrete facts of experience whereas the latter goes beyond them. As Pratab Chandra points out:

> *"The Upaniṣads seldom care for actual experiences; their aim is to discover a suprasensuous, supraphenomenal reality, entirely free from change and the laws of the world ... Psychological analysis may not be absent in the Upaniṣads, but it hardly forms any significant part of them. Early Buddhism, on the contrary, uncompromisingly refuses to transcend the empirical..."*[137]

From this it follows that the disagreement between the Upaniṣadic thinkers and the Buddha on the problem of the self is partly due to the different methods they employ: the former, practising Yoga, propound the *ātman* theory, while the latter, practising *vipassanā* meditation, advocates the *anattā* theory.

## PROBLEMS

In preaching the *anattā* doctrine, the Buddha claims to have avoided the two extreme views, namely, eternalism and annihilationism. Unlike the eternalists such as the Upaniṣadic thinkers, the Buddha rejects the existence of the permanent self. And, unlike the nihilists, such as Ajita Kesakambala, the Buddha accepts the doctrine of *karma* and rebirth. His 'middle' position, however, constitutes some major problems. How can one reconcile the *anattā* doctrine, which denies the permanent self, with the doctrine of karma and rebirth, which seems to presuppose the identity and continuity of the person? Is it possible to talk of personal identity and unity of consciousness without having recourse to the notion of the permanent self? Since the solution of these problems is related to the conception of consciousness, in the next chapter we shall first consider the nature of consciousness in Buddhism and then return to the solutions of these and other problems.

## NOTES

1 S.XXII. 59.
2 M.I. 380.
3 T.W. Rhys Davids, *Dialogues of the Buddha*, Part 1, PTS, 1899, p. 242.
4 Nyanatiloka, *Buddhist Dictionary*, BPS, Kandy, 1980, p. 14.
5 D.I. Sutta No. 1.
6 Kvu. 62.
7 S. XIII. 35.
8 BN. 682.
9 D.I. 55.
10 Sarvadarsana-saṁgraha, 2.
11 M.I. 136; S. XXII, 81.
12 Deussen, P., *The Philosophy of the Upanishads*, Oriental Books Reprint, 1979, p. 39.
13 Ṛg-Veda. X. 16.3.
14 Radhakrishnan, S., *The Principal Upaniṣads*, George Allen and Unwin Ltd., London, 1974, p. 73.
15 Chānd. Up. VIII. 8. 1.
16 Māṇḍ. Up. VIII.
17 Chānd. Up. VIII. 12.1

18 Bṛh. Up. III 7. 20.
19 Quoted by S. Radhakrishnan in *Indian Philosophy*, Vol.I, George Allen and Unwin, 1983, p. 159.
20 Bṛh. Up. IV 5.6.
21 Bṛh. Up. II. 4.14; IV. 5.15.
22 Bṛh. Up. III. 4.2.
23 Chānd. Up. VI. 12.1.
24 Bṛh. Up. IV. 5.15.
25 Radhakrishnan, S., *The Principal Upaniṣads*, p. 69.
26 Deussen, P., op. cit, p. 42.
27 Kathā Up. 1. 3, 12.
28 Radhakrishnan, S. *The Principal Upaniṣads*, p. 646.
29 Muṇḍ. Up. III. 2.8.
30 James, W., *The Varieties of Religious Experience*, Modern Library, 1929, p. 391.
31 Radhakrishnan, S., *Indian Philosophy*, Vol. I, p. 176.
32 Inge, *Plotinus*, Vol. II, p. 140.
33 Tait. Up. 1. 511.
34 Tait. Up. II. 8.1
35 Chānd. Up. VI. 8. 7f.
36 Bṛh. Up. I. 4.10.
37 Muṇḍ. Up. III. 2.9.
38 Deussen, P. op. cit., p. 346.
39 Muṇḍ. Up. III. 2.8-9.
40 Husserl, E., *Ideas*, Tr. by W.R. Boyce Gibson, George Allen and Unwin Ltd., 1969, s. 57, p. 173.
41 *Ideas*, s. 80, p. 233 and Mānd. Up. VIII.
42 *Ideas*, s. 80, p 233.
43 *Ideas*, p. 51.
44 Husserl, E., *Cartesian Meditations*, Tr. by Dorion Cairns, Martinus Nijhoff, 1977, s. 11, p. 26.
45 *Ideas*, p. 18.
46 Radhakrishnan S., *The Principal Upaniṣads*, p. 69.
47 Puligandla, R., "Phenomenological Reduction and Yogic Meditation", *Philosophy East and West*, Vol. XX, No. I, 1970 p. 22.
48 Koestenbaum, P., "Religion in the Tradition of Phenomenology", in *Religion in Philosophical and Cultural Perspective*, ed. by J. C. Feaner and W. Horosz, D. Van Nostrand Company Inc., 1967, p. 187.
49 De Silva, L. A., *The Problem of the Self in Buddhism and Christianity*, The Study Centre for Religion and Society, 1975, p. 25.
50 Jayatilleke, K. N., *Early Buddhist Theory of Knowledge*, Motilal Banarsidass, Delhi, 1980 p. 65.
51 M.I. 8.
52 D. II. 307.
53 S. XXII. 56.
54 Vism. Ch. XIV, p. 460.
55 Buddhaghosa, *The Expositor (Atthasālinī)*, tr. by Pe Maung Tin, Oxford

University Press, London, 1958, p. 145.
56 S. XXXVI. 1.
57 S. X. II. 56.
58 M.I. 293.
59 Rhys Davids, C. A. F., *A Buddhist Manual of Psychological Ethics (Dhammasaṅganī)*, Oriental Books Reprint Corpn., 1975, p. 7, n. 2.
60 S. XXII. 56.
61 Vism. Ch. XIV. p. 452.
62 Rahula, W., *What the Buddha Taught*, Grove Press, Inc., 1962, p. 23.
63 S. XXII. 56.
64 De Silva, P., *Buddhist and Freudian Psychology*, Lake House Investment Ltd., 1973 p. 7.
65 Flügel, J.C. *Studies in Feeling and Desire*, Duckworth, London, 1955, p. 49.
66 Narada, *A Manual of Abhidhamma*, B.P.S., Kandy, 1975, p. 76.
67 Nyanatiloka, *Buddhist Dictionary*, p. 100.
68 M.I. 293.
69 Bṛh. Up. III, 7. 16-22.
70 S. XXII, 59.
71 Vism. Ch. XXI. p. 640.
72 M.I. 232-233; S. XXII, 79.
73 M.I. 136.
74 Chānd. Up. VIII. 8-12.
75 Hume. D., *A Treatise of Human Nature*, Oxford, 1975, p. 252.
76 Ibid. pp. 252-3.
77 S.V. 10.
78 Vism. Ch. XVIII. p. 593-4.
79 S.XXII. 45.
80 Vism. Ch. XX. pp. 611-612.
81 Dhammapada, Ch. XX, 277-78-79.
*" Sabbe saṅkhārā aniccā...*
*Sabbe saṅkhārā dukkhā...*
*Sabbe dhammā anattā...."*
82 Rhys Davids, T.W., *Early Buddhism*, Bharatiya Publishing House, 1976, p. 56.
83 S. XXII. 90.
84 M. III. 63; S. XII. 21.
85 To put it into a modern form:
When A is, B is;
A arising, B arises;
When A is not, B is not;
A ceasing, B ceases
86 M.III. 63-4 and elsewhere.
87 Vism. Ch. XVII. p. 517.
88 M.I. 54.
89 S. XII. 20.
90 S. XII. 20.

91 S.XXII. 18-20.
92 Vism. Ch. XIX. p. 513.
93 Vism. Ch. XVI., p. 513.
94 James, W., *The Principles of Psychology,* Vol. 1. Dover Publications Inc. 1950, p 401.
95 BN. 246.
96 S. XII. 35.
97 Malalasekera. G P. *The Truth of Anattā,* BPS, 1966, p 25.
98 Nyanatiloka, *Egolessness (Anattā),* BPS, 1974, p. 3.
99 S. XXII. 96.
100 M.I. 137.
101 D.II. 305. *"Saṅkhittena pañcupādānakkhandhā dukkhā."*
102 M.I. 51; S. XXII. 83.
103 See above. p. 37.
104 James, W., op. cit., p. 317.
105 Fromm, E., *The Heart of Man,* London, 1965, p.88.
106 M.I. 6.
107 S. XXII. 83.
108 D. III. 273.
109 S. XXII. 125.
110 S. XXII. 47.
111 M.I. 7.
112 Horner, I. B., *The Middle Length Sayings,* Vol. I, PTS., London, 1976. p. 9 n. 2.
113 A.II. 51.
114 Vism. Ch. XXI. p. 640.
115 See above. p 40.
116 S. XXII. 81.
117 M.III. 63.
118 M.I. 300.
119 M.I. 48, 299; III. 250.
120 De Silva, P., *Buddhist and Freudian Psychology,* p. 73.
121 See above, p. 85.
122 Iti. II. 12.
123 Rahula, W. op. cit. p. 69.
124 Jayatilleke, K.N., *Early Buddhist Theory of Knowledge,* pp. 169, 451.
125 M.II. 211.
126 De Silva, P., *An Introduction to Buddhist Psychology,* The MacMillan Press Ltd., 1979, p. 13.
127 S. III. 44.
128 Nyanatiloka, *Buddhist Dictionary,* p. 36.
129 Vism. Ch. III, p. 85.
130 S. XII. 23.
131 D. Sutta n. 22.
132 A.V. 3, 313.
133 Sinari, R., "The Method of Phenomenological Reduction and Yoga", *Philosophy East and West,* Vol. 15, No. 3, 1965, p. 226.

134 See above, p. 98.
135 M. I. 41.
136 Nyanatiloka, *The Word of the Buddha*, BPS, 1968, p. 79.
137 Pratab Chandra, "Was Early Buddhism Influenced by the Upaniṣads?", *Philosophy East and West*, Vol. XXI, No. 3, 1971, p. 323.

# IV

# THE BUDDHIST CONCEPTION OF CONSCIOUSNESS

We have seen in our discussion on the Buddhist's rejection of the self that the person *(puggala)* consists of five aggregates, viz. corporeality, feeling, perception, mental formations, and consciousness. Our attention in this chapter will be focused on the aggregate of consciousness *(viññāṇa)*, which is one of the four nonmaterial aggregates. The five aggregates can be divided into two main groups, the material and the nonmaterial. The aggregate of corporeality belongs to the material group called *'rūpa'* (form). The term *'rūpa'* specifies the bodily constituent of the personality. "The *attabhāvo*, or personality, *minus* all mental and moral characteristics, is *rūpaṁ*."[1] The remaining aggregates, i.e. feeling, perception, mental formations, and consciousness, belong to the nonmaterial group called *'nāma'* (name). The term *'nāma'* is used to refer to all mental phenomena. "Thus the aggregate of corporeality," writes Buddhaghosa, "is form (*rūpa*), the four nonmaterial aggregates are name (*nāma*)."[2] Name and form taken together constitute the psycho-physical complex known as person (*puggala*).

In the *Abhidhamma,* it should be noted, the term *'nāma'* is extended to include not only the four nonmaterial aggregates but also *Nirvāṇa.*[3] Here the nonmaterial aggregates are considered under two terms: *'citta'* (consciousness) and *'cetasika'* (psychic factor). The term *'citta'* is said to be a synonym for two other terms, namely, *viññāṇa* (consciousness) and *mana* (mind)[4] whereas the term *'cetasika'* is used to refer to the remaining nonmaterial aggregates, viz. feeling, perception and mental formations. *Citta* and *cetasika* are two of the four ultimate categories *(paramattha)* with which the *Abhidhamma* is concerned, the other two being *rūpa* (matter) and *Nirvāṇa.* [5]

## FIFTY-TWO PSYCHIC FACTORS

The aggregates of feeling, perception and mental formations are called psychic factors *(cetasika)* because they are associated with consciousness (*citta*).[6] In the *Abhidhammatthasaṅgaha,* Anuruddha has given a clear and precise definition of psychic factors: "Psychic factors are those that arise and perish together with consciousness, are associated with consciousness and share the same object and basis with consciousness."[7] There are altogether fifty-two psychic factors, two of which are feeling and perception. The remaining fifty are mental formations *(saṅkhāra).* The fifty-two psychic factors are distributed under three distinct basic classes, each class consisting of two subclasses as follows:

1. General psychic factors: (a) primary and (b) secondary.
2. Unwholesome psychic factors: (a) primary and (b) secondary.
3. Wholesome psychic factors: (a) primary and (b) secondary.

1. (a) General psychic factors (*sabbacittasādhāraṇa-cetasika*) are

seven in number: contact *(phassa)*, feeling *(vedanā)*, perception (*saññā*), intention *(cetanā)* one-pointedness *(ekaggatā)*, psychic vitality *(jīvitindriya)* and attention *(manasikāra)*. These seven factors are common to every act of consciousness.

(b) The secondary psychic factors are six in number: initial application *(vitakka)*, sustained application *(vicāra)*, decision (*adhimokkha*), effort *(viriya)*, rapture *(pīti)*, and active urge *(chanda)*.

These factors are not found in all types of consciousness, thus they are called the "particulars" *(pakiṇṇaka)*.

2. (a) The primary unwholesome *(akusala)* factors found invariably in all classes of unwholesome consciousness are four in number: delusion (*moha*), lack of moral shame *(ahirika)*, lack of moral dread *(anottappa)* and restlessness *(uddhacca)*.

(b) The secondary unwholesome factors are ten in number: hatred *(dosa)*, envy *(issā)*, selfishness *(macchariya)*, worry *(kukkucca)*, greed (*lobha*), wrong view (*diṭṭhi*), conceit *(māna)*, sloth (*thīna*), torpor (*middha*) and doubt *(vicikicchā)*. These factors do not occur in all unwholesome classes of consciousness.

3. (a) The primary wholesome *(kusala)* factors are common to all classes of wholesome consciousness. The wholesome is also beautiful. Hence these factors are called the "beautiful universal" *(sobhaṇasādhāraṇa)*. These factors are nineteen in number: faith *(saddhā)*, mindfulness (*sati*), shame *(hiri)*, moral dread *(ottappa)*, non-greed *(alobha)*, non-hatred *(adosa)*, equanimity *(tatramajjhattatā)*, calmness of psychic factors *(kāyapassaddhi)*, calmness of consciousness *(cittapassaddhi)*, buoyancy of psychic factors *(lahutā)*, buoyancy of consciousness, pliancy of psychic factors *(mudutā)*, pliancy of consciousness, fitness of psychic factors *(kammaññatā)*, fitness of consciousness, proficiency of psychic factors *(pāguññatā)*, proficiency of consciousness, rectitude of psychic factors *(ujukatā)*, and rectitude of consciousness.

(b) The secondary wholesome factors found in some classes of wholesome consciousness are six in number: right speech *(sammā-vācā)*, right action *(sammā-kammanta)*, right livelihood *(sammā-ājīva)*, compassion *(karuṇā)*, sympathetic joy *(muditā)*, and wisdom (*paññā*).[8]

## CONTENTS OF CONSCIOUSNESS

The psychic factors described above accompany consciousness. Thus consciousness does not arise in isolation; it always arises together with a number of psychic factors. Consciousness and psychic factors, though external to one another in analysis, are in reality intimately and inseparably connected with one another. "Consciousness and psychic factors are related to one another by way of association *(sampayuttapaccaya)*."[9] Hence consciousness in its purest form does not function in utter isolation and separation; it is always accompanied by some psychic factors. This means that consciousness, in spite of being egoless, is not contentless because it has psychic factors as its contents. And in so far as it contains *something*, consciousness cannot be regarded as nothingness *(natthitā)*. It is "consciousness-and-something-more." Consciousness is said to be wholesome *(kusala)* or unwholesome *(akusala)* according to its contents, i.e. psychic factors.

Consciousness is defined by intentionality; that is, consciousness is consciousness of an object.[10] The relation between subject *(ārammaṇika)* and object *(ārammaṇa)* is called *phassa* (contact), which is similar to the notion of intentionality in phenomenology. Consciousness, however, is related to its object with the help of six sense-organs *(dvāra* or *āyatana)*, viz. eye, ear, nose, tongue, body and mind. "Whatever one sees through the eye, hears through the ear, smells through the nose, touches through the body, recognizes through the mind—all these one knows by consciousness."[11] Thus the triad of *consciousness, sense-organ* and *object* is accepted in early Buddhism. "The coming together of the three is contact *(phassa)*."[12]

## SELF-CONSCIOUSNESS

It should be noted here that the early Buddhist accepts mind-door (*manodvāra*) as the "sixth" sense, in addition to the five physical sense organs of which visible object, sound, odor, taste, and tangible thing are their objects. The sixth sense has all mental phenomena as its objects,[13] and it is through this sixth inner sense that consciousness can reflect upon itself and its psychic factors. Without the mind-door, consciousness cannot know itself, just as a person without eye-door *(cakkhudvāra)* cannot see visible objects. Through this mind-door, consciousness knows itself as an object, not as a subject. That is, consciousness by nature is not self-conscious; it is not implicitly aware of itself when it is aware of an object.[14] Consciousness can only be aware of one object at one time. "When we attend to present things, we are not able at the present moment to attend to the consciousness by which they arise."[15] This is because consciousness "cannot be subject and object at once."[16] Just as one cannot cut a sword with that very same sword, an axe with that axe, and a knife with that knife, so also one cannot know consciousness with that very same consciousness.[17]

It is interesting to note here that the Vijñāṇavādin of Mahāyāna Buddhism holds a different view from the Theravādin. According to the Vijñāṇavādin, "every consciousness and every mental phenomenon is self conscious."[18] Knowledge is self-luminous (*svayam-prakāṣa*). Just as a lamp illumines the neighboring objects and its own self at the same time, so also consciousness is aware of its object and itself at one and the same moment. Nevertheless the Mādhyamika does not agree with the Vijñāṇavādin. The former says that consciousness, being empty, cannot know itself. "Even the sharpest sword cannot cut itself; the fingertips cannot be touched by the same fingertips. Consciousness does not know itself."[19] In this respect the Mādhyamika's position is not different from the Theravādin's.

## THE MATERIAL OBJECT

Now we have seen that consciousness in early Buddhism is defined as that which is conscious of an object *(ārammaṇa)*. Here the term *'ārammaṇa'* (object) is to be understood in the sense of *'ālambitabba,'* which means that which is hung upon by consciousness.[20] Without an object to be 'hung upon,' consciousness cannot arise. Hence object is one of the necessary conditions for the arising of consciousness. Buddhaghosa writes:

> *"Eye-consciousness arises due to eye, visible object, light, and attention ... Ear-consciousness arises due to ear, sound, aperture, and attention ... Mind-consciousness arises due to subconsciousness, mental object, and attention."*[21]

Since it is born supported or conditioned by the object, consciousness cannot exist without an object. From the fact that greater prominence is given to the object, Buddhism cannot be classed as idealism. "Early Buddhism," writes Jayatilleke, "is *realistic* in that it held matter *(rūpa)* to non-mental *(acetasikaṁ)* and independent of thought *(citta-vippayutta)*."[22] Unlike Berkeley, the Buddhist thinks that the existence of the material object does not depend on its being perceived. The material object, however, exists in the state of perpetual flux or becoming. It is impermanent *(anicca)*. *Rūpa* (matter) in Buddhism is not defined as the extended thing *(res extensa)*, but as "the changeable thing" *(ruppatīti rūpaṁ)*.[23] The material object, as we shall see, arises and perishes every moment. It is momentary *(khaṇika)*. The object, however, appears as relatively permanent due to the meaning-giving activity of consciousness. Consciousness is called 'name' *(nāma)* because it has a tendency to "name" the object,[24] i.e. to constitute the meaning of the world.

## THE PHENOMENAL WORLD

According to Buddhism, the objects of our sensory impression (*paṭigha-samphassa*) are momentary and non-substantial, but their true nature is distorted when they are conceptualized by our consciousness influenced by lust (*rāga*), hatred (*dosa*) and delusion (*moha*).[25] And due to conceptualization by consciousness, the phenomenal world is constituted. The psychological process which constitutes the world has been described in the Madhupiṇḍika-Sutta:

> *"Whatever man perceives* (sañjānāti*) that he conceives* (vitakketi*); whatever he conceives that he differentiates* (papañceti*); and what he differentiates, by reason thereof ideas and considerations of differentiation* (papañca-saññā-saṅkhā*) arise in him."*[26]

In this statement the term *'papañca'* refers to the differentiation or manifoldness of the world.[27] The opposite term *'nippapañca'* is a name for *Nirvāṇa* or the end of the world. The *Arahant* is the person whose concept of the world disappears: "Mankind delights in the manifoldness of the world, the Perfect Ones are free from such manifoldness."[28] This is because the *Arahant*'s consciousness limits itself to what is 'given'; it does not impose meaning on the thing perceived. The Buddha says: "In the seen, there will be just the seen; in the heard, just the heard; in the sensed, just the sensed; in the cognized, just the cognized."[29] Again, "Regard the world as empty (*suñña*), Mogharāja, and be always mindful: thus will you be able to overcome death!"[30] But, unlike the *Arahant*, the ordinary person (*puthujjana*) constitutes the phenomenal world and clings to it. He has distortions (*vipallāsa*) of perception, thought and view. Referring to this "constituted" phenomenal world, the Buddha says:

> *"In this body of six foot height with its perception and its consciousness, is contained the world, the arising of the world, the end of the world, and the way that leads to the end of the world."*[31]

We should make it clear that when we say that consciousness constitutes the world, we do not mean that consciousness idealistically creates the material world; what we want to say is that consciousness constitutes the *meaning* of the phenomenal world. And the meaning thus constituted is regarded as conventional truth (*sammuti-sacca*), whereas the true nature of things prior to constitution represents the ultimate truth (*paramattha-sacca*). Accordingly, the Buddha makes two kinds of statements, viz. conventional and absolute. "A conventional statement is true because of convention and an absolute statement is true as (disclosing) the true characteristics of things."[32] Such terms as 'person' (*puggala*), 'living being' (*satta*) and 'self' (*attā*) form parts of the conventional statement, and such terms as 'impermanent' (*anicca*), 'suffering' (*dukkha*) and 'selflessness' (*anattā*) form parts of the absolute statement.[33]

## MOMENTARINESS

The consciousness which gives meaning to the world is by nature momentary (*khaṇika*); it arises and perishes in each and every moment. Consciousness can never remain the same for any two consecutive moments. Each moment of consciousness is extremely short. The Buddha says: "I consider, monks, that there is no phenomenon that comes and goes so quickly as consciousness. It is not easy to find a simile to show how quickly consciousness comes and goes."[34] In the Saṁyutta-Nikāya, the Buddha compares the phenomenon of consciousness with the quick movements of a monkey:

> *"Just as a monkey, monks, faring through the dense forest catches one bough and, letting it go, catches another, and then another; even so, monks, that which we call mind* (citta)*, thought* (mano)*, consciousness* (viññāṇa)*, that arises as one thing, ceases as another, both by night and by day."*[35]

Every moment of consciousness is subdivided into three sub-moments, namely, genesis *(uppāda)*, development (*ṭhiti*) and dissolution (*bhaṅga*).[36] Each of these sub-moments occupies an infinitesimal division of time so that to every separate act of consciousness *(cittuppāda)* there are three phases, in which successively it arises, develops and disappears. These three sub-moments together form one conscious moment *(cittakkhaṇa)*, the period occupied by any single act of consciousness. According to the Commentators of the Pali Canon, there are more than one billion such conscious moments in the time that would be occupied by the shortest flash of lightning.[37]

Moments of consciousness, short-lived as they are, succeed

one another so rapidly that they appear to be 'the stream of consciousness' (*viññāṇa-sota*)[38] which perpetually flows "like the current of a river" *(nadīsoto viya)*.[39] The current of a river maintains one constant form, one seeming identity, though not a single drop of water remains today of all the volume that composed that river yesterday.[40] In like manner, the stream of consciousness appears to be selfsame, though not a single act of consciousness remains the same for any two consecutive moments.

## THE UNITY OF CONSCIOUSNESS

Now some questions arise: Since acts of consciousness last for a very short time, how can they form a stream of consciousness? What combines these conscious acts in such a way that there arises the selfsame stream of experience? In other words, what is the unifying principle of consciousness? The Buddhist, having rejected the permanent self, cannot accept that there exists in consciousness a permanent entity which functions as the unifying principle of consciousness. He has to admit, as Sartre does, that consciousness unifies itself.

According to the Buddhist, acts of consciousness are causally related to one another according to the natural uniformity of consciousness *(cittaniyāma)*. Each conscious act has causal relation with its predecessor. Twenty-four modes of causal relation *(paccaya)* are enumerated and explained in the *Paṭṭhāna*, the last book of the *Abhidhamma-Piṭaka*. Of these twenty-four, four modes of conditionality are applied to the relation between two conscious acts. As Anuruddha points out in the *Abhidhammatthasaṅgaha:*

> *"Consciousness and psychic factors that immediately cease, relate themselves to present consciousness and psychic factors by way of contiguity* (anantara), *immediacy* (samanantara), *absence* (natthi), *and disappearance* (vigata)*."*[41]

By way of contiguity and immediacy, one conscious moment

perishes immediately giving birth to another. The succeeding conscious moment inherits all the potentialities of its immediate predecessor. The present conscious moment is also related to the preceding moment in the modes of absence and disappearance. That is, with the absence and disappearance of the predecessor, the successor appears. For instance, the visual consciousness *(dassana)* is causally related to the immediately following receiving consciousness (*sampaṭicchana*) by way of absence and disappearance. S.Z. Aung writes:

> *"This fourfold correlation is understood to mean that each expired state renders service* (upakāra) *to the next. In other words, each, on passing away, gives up the whole of the energy* (paccaya-satti) *to its successor. Each successor, therefore, has all the potentialities of its predecessors, and more."*[42]

It is these four causal relations that make the unity and continuity of conscious acts possible. Although the stream of consciousness remains the same, conscious acts which succeed one another in that stream are not identical. The present conscious act is not absolutely the same as its immediate predecessor because the former arises immediately after the disappearance of the latter. Nor is the present conscious act entirely different from its immediate predecessor because the former inherits all the potentialities of the latter. Thus in the same stream of consciousness there is continuity (*santati*), but no identity (*ekatā*). Any two consecutive moments of consciousness are, in Nāgasena's words, "neither the same nor different" (*na ca so, na ca añño*). [43]

## THE PERSONAL IDENTITY

One question may be raised here: If it is true that there is no absolute identity in the stream of consciousness, how does the Buddhist explain the sense of personal identity? What exactly enables me to say that I am the same man that I was yesterday? The Buddhist would say that there is no permanent self underlying the ever-changing stream of experience. For the Buddhist, it is nothing but the continuity of memory that gives rise to the sense of personal identity. By inheriting all the potentialities from its predecessors, consciousness is accumulative; nothing is really forgotten.[44] With all its heritage of the past, consciousness recognizes an object in the image reproduced, or the idea revived, of the original object by the very marks which were observed by its predecessors in a certain perception or reflection. Thus the remembering consciousness "has come to regard the image as the copy, and the idea as the counterpart, of the original object intuited or reflected upon."[45]

A. J. Ayer, like the Buddhist, thinks that "some continuity of memory is necessary" for the possibility of personal identity.[46] Given a series of experiences, we must thread them together by assuming that later experiences consist partly in recollections of their predecessors. Ayer writes: "If we want to enlist every member of the series, we shall have to assume that each of them is related to at least one of the others either actively or passively with respect to memory."[47] But this would mean that every experience is related to previous memories. The question now is: What is the relation between two items of experience? Ayer then concludes that memory is not sufficient for maintaining self-identity because it needs to be backed by some other relation of which "nothing more illuminating can be said than that it is the relation that holds between experiences."[48] Thus his difficulty is due to the fact that he has not succeeded in discovering the relation between two items of experience. Hume has had the same problem. He holds the view that the self is "a bundle of perceptions." Hume, however, has not been able to show adequately what it is that integrates or orders the bundle. His difficulty has its root in two principles which he accepted and could neither renounce nor reconcile—"that all our distinct perceptions are distinct existences" and "that the mind never perceives any real connection among distinct existences."[49] Distinct perceptions are distinct existences inasmuch as any one of them can exist even though the others have no existence. In this sense, Humean perception appears to be a being-in-itself, in

Sartre's terminology. For Sartre, the relation between two perceptions is unsuccessfully accounted for in Hume's atomistic framework. "Any connection with an antecedent or a consequent, no matter how constant it may be, remains unintelligible."[50]

## THE CAUSAL RELATION

The Buddhist admits that there is a difficulty in apprehending the causal relation. The Buddha says: "Deep is this doctrine of causal arising, and it looks deep too."[51] As is mentioned earlier, the causal relation in Buddhism is not subjective and it is not a category imposed by consciousness on its objects. The causal relation is "objective reality" (*tathatā*)[52] and is denoted by the term *'dhammatā,'* which literally means "the nature of things." Thus it is said:

> *"It is in the nature of things (*dhammatā*) that the* absence of remorse *is present in a virtuous person. A person who has no (feeling of) remorse need not determine in his mind that* joy *should arise in him. It is of the nature of things that joy arises in a person who lacks remorse. A person who is joyful need not determine in his mind that* delight *should arise in him. It is of the nature of things that delight arises in a joyful person."*[53]

This passage clearly shows how moments of consciousness succeed one another. That is, with the absence (*natthi*) and disappearance (*vigata-paccaya*) of remorse-consciousness, joy-consciousness arises. And joy-consciousness, on passing away, transmits all the potentialities to delight-consciousness which immediately follows it (*anantara-, samanantara-paccaya*). This causal relation is in the nature of things (*dhammatā*). Here the term 'the nature of things' (*dhammatā*) refers to the causal psychological processes.[54] Now we can see a difference between the Buddhist and Hume on the ontological status of causal relation. The Buddhist thinks that causal relation is objectively real whereas Hume holds the view that the causal relation is subjective and based on habit. According to Hume, our mind is in the habit of experiencing certain effects from certain causes. The external events are related by this operation of mind, which trusts in the uniformity of nature.

Furthermore, the Buddhist differs from Hume in that the former does not regard conscious acts, or perceptions in the Humean sense, as "distinct existences." For the Buddhist each act of consciousness cannot exist without relation to some causes: *"Apart from conditions there is no arising of consciousness."*[55] Consciousness is not a substantial, static entity. It is not a being-in-itself; rather it is a becoming (*bhava*). Each conscious moment is by nature causally related to its predecessor and successor. As we have already seen, the present moment of consciousness is subdivided into three sub-moments, namely, genesis, development and dissolution. At the instant of genesis, consciousness is generated by the potentialities of the perishing consciousness; it is born an owner of all the contents of the predecessor. In other words, it is a 'retention' of the past. Then comes the submoment of development. At this instant, consciousness is not influenced by the past, but by the external object (*ārammaṇa-paccaya*) and the internal force of intention (*cetanā*). The two factors produce *karma*-energy. At the instant of dissolution, the present consciousness, on passing away, transmits *karma*-energy and other potentialities to its immediate successor; it is a 'projection' into the future. Here we find that the submoments of genesis and dissolution are analogous to the Husserlian acts of 'retention' and 'protention.'

## WILLIAM JAMES ON THE STREAM OF CONSCIOUSNESS

It is interesting to note that the Buddhist theory of the causal relation between two conscious moments can be likened to William James' theory of the relation between thought-moments. Like the Buddhist, James uses the words "stream of consciousness" to refer to the continuous flow of mental phenomena. Explaining why he calls it such, James writes:

*"Such words as 'chain' or 'train' do not describe it fitly as it presents itself in the first instance. It is nothing joined; it flows. A 'river' and a 'stream' are metaphors by which it is most naturally described. In talking of it hereafter, let us call it the stream of thought, of consciousness, or of subjective life."*[56]

Again, like the Buddhist, James rejects the existence of the substantial self or soul.[57] The postulate of the self is not necessary for the unity of consciousness.

*"The unity, the identity, the individuality, and the immateriality that appear in the psychic life are thus accounted for as phenomenal and temporal facts exclusively, and with no need of reference to any more simple or substantial agent than the present thought or 'section' of the stream."*[58]

At any given moment, the active source of unification is "the real, present onlooking, remembering, 'judging thought' ..."[59] The judging thought, as a 'section' of the stream, is momentary. This thought-moment is counted as conscious moment *(cittakhaṇa)* in Buddhist terminology. James then explains how thought moments are united. His explanation, it should be noted, is not different from the Buddhist version described above.

According to James, the preceding thought, on passing away, transmits its whole energy to its successor. The contents are passed on from one thought to the next in a continuous succession. James writes:

*"Each pulse of cognitive consciousness, each Thought, dies away and is replaced by another. The other, among the things it knows, knows its own predecessor, and finding it 'warm,' in the way we have described, greets it, saying, 'Thou art mine, and part of the same self with me.'"*[60]

Each thought, knowing and appropriating its predecessors, is the final owner. Each thought is thus born an owner, and dies owned, transmitting its properties to its own later proprietors.

> *"As Kant says, it is as if elastic balls were to have not only motion but knowledge of it, and a first ball were to transmit both its motion and its consciousness to a second, which took both up into its consciousness and passed them to a third, until the last ball held all that the other balls had held, and realized as its own."*[61]

James' description gives us an insight into the Buddhist theory of the unity and continuity of consciousness. It shows how egoless consciousness unifies itself: The permanent self is rendered useless for the unity and continuity of the stream of consciousness.

We have already seen that consciousness in Buddhism is momentary and moments of consciousness are causally related to one another. The unity and continuity of consciousness are effected, not by the permanent self *(attā)*, but by the causal relations of contiguity, immediacy, absence and disappearance. Moments of consciousness, thus related, succeed one another with inconceivable rapidity and thereby constitute the stream of consciousness *(viññāṇa-sota)*. The stream of consciousness flows on uninterruptedly like the current of a river until the moment of death.[62]

## SUBCONSCIOUSNESS

Here one question arises: If the flow of consciousness never stops, what happens to consciousness when man is in deep, dreamless sleep? According to Radhakrishnan, *suṣupti* or deep sleep is a normal occurrence of man's life. "In it the mind and the sense are both said to be inactive."[63] Does it mean that the stream of consciousness stops flowing during dreamless sleep? The Buddhist's answer is in the negative. According to him, the consciousness of someone in dreamless sleep continues to flow in the state of *bhavaṅga*. As Nāgasena has pointed out in the *Milindapañhā:*

*"When someone is in deep sleep, his mind is in the* bhavaṅga *state; a mind in the* bhavaṅga *state does not function, and a mind inactive knows not the evil and the good, and he who knows not does not dream. For it is when a mind is active that dreams are dreamt."*[64]

What, then, is this *bhavaṅga?*

By *bhavaṅga* is meant "the cause, reason, indispensable condition, of our being regarded subjectively as continuous; the *sine qua non* of our existence, that without which one cannot subsist or exist."[65] *Bhavaṅga* is a function of our being; it makes the passive side of our existence possible. It denotes a functional state of subconsciousness. "As such it is the subconscious state of mind—'below the threshold' of consciousness—by which we conceive continuous subjective existence as possible."[66] In this sense, *bhavaṅga* is nothing but consciousness (*viññāṇa*) which has no possibility of knowing itself. As is mentioned earlier, consciousness is not self-conscious. But consciousness can know itself as an object through the mind-door (*manodvāra*) or the inner sense; that is, it can be known by reflection or introspection only. And consciousness can be reflected upon only when it is active in the sense of coming into contact with external or internal objects through any one of the six doors (*dvāra*) or channels (*āpatha*), namely, eye, ear, nose, tongue, body and mind. The active consciousness is called 'processed consciousness' (*vīthicitta*) as it functions through the process which we will consider later on. It is this processed consciousness that can be the object of reflection. But the passive 'process-freed consciousness' (*vīthi-mutta*) can never be reflected upon because it is below the mind-door or 'threshold of consciousness' (*manodvāra*). Since it cannot be known by reflection, the process-freed consciousness is called *bhavaṅga* or subconsciousness. And the dividing-line between subconsciousness and processed consciousness (*vīthi-citta*) is the threshold of consciousness (*manodvāra*).[67]

Thus consciousness does not stop during the period of dreamless sleep; the subconscious state of consciousness flows on without interruption. This subconscious stream is arrested when the process-freed consciousness makes contact (*phassa*) with an object through the sense doors. When a material object (*rūpārammaṇa*) is presented to consciousness through one of the five sense-doors, a processed consciousness (*vīthicitta*) arises, consisting of a series of separate conscious moments succeeding one another in a particular uniform order. This order is known as psychic order (*citta-niyāma*).[68] In order to have a complete perception of the material object, consciousness must have passed through seventeen consecutive moments. If the series for some reason is incomplete, the perception does not attain clearness. For this reason, a moment of material object is said to correspond to seventeen conscious moments.[69] These seventeen conscious moments are as follows:

1. past subconsciousness (*atīta-bhavaṅga*),
2. disturbance of subconsciousness (*bhavaṅga-calana*),
3. subconsciousness cut off (*bhavaṅga-upaccheda*),
4. advertence through one of the five sense-doors (*pañcadvārāvajjana*),
5. consciousness through one of the five senses (*pañcaviññāṇa*),
6. reception (*sampaṭicchana*),
7. examination (*santīraṇa*),
8. determining (*voṭṭhapana*),

9-15. impulsions (*javana*),

16-17. registering (*tadārammaṇa*). [70]

Since our main concern here is to understand the nature of subconsciousness (*bhavaṅga-viññāṇa*), we shall not go into details about these seventeen moments. For the present purpose, the series may be divided into four sections. Firstly, moments *one* to *three* represent the initial entry of the perceptual object into the receptive medium of consciousness, and the disturbance as well as the arrest of subconscious stream caused by that entry. Second, moments *four* to *eight* represent a gradually increasing attention to the object, in which its particular nature and qualities are received, examined and determined. Third, moments *nine* to *fifteen* represent the full cognition of the object. Lastly, moments *sixteen* to *seventeen* represent a 'registering' of the perception as a whole; they may be viewed as the transition from a perception to a primary memory. After the last two moments perish, there is "the subsidence into the subconscious state" (*bhavaṅga-pāto*).[71]

## SUBCONSCIOUSNESS AND THE TRANSCENDENTAL EGO

Out of these seventeen conscious moments, the first is subconsciousness or process-freed consciousness. The remaining sixteen moments represent the processed consciousness. This processed consciousness appears to have subconsciousness or *bhavaṅga* as its origin. "*Bhavaṅga* is that from which all thought processes emerge when necessary conditions are present."[72] And for this reason, Buddhaghosa regards subconsciousness as "the condition of active consciousness."[73] In this sense, subconsciousness *(bhavaṅga)* is similar to the transcendental ego which, according to Husserl, is the origin of conscious acts. Thus subconsciousness may be viewed as a functional substitute for the transcendental ego as well as the substantial self *(ātman)* in Buddhist thought.[74] The Buddhist, however, would not accept the view that subconsciousness is a self in disguise. The self or ego is not liable to change, but subconsciousness changes every moment.

> *"Like any other consciousness it (*bhavaṅga*) also consists of three aspects—genesis (*uppāda*), static (*ṭhiti*) and cessation (*bhaṅga*). Arising and perishing every moment it flows on like a stream not remaining the same for two consecutive moments."*[75]

Hence subconsciousness is a type of consciousness *(viññāṇa)* which is passive or process-freed; it is conscious of its object without passing through the process (*vīthi*). The object of the process-freed consciousness is the former object of the processed consciousness; it is taken along when the latter subsides into the subconscious state. Thus subconsciousness is not objectless or contentless. It inherits all the contents of the processed consciousness.

From the foregoing discussion it is clear that consciousness does not stop flowing during dreamless sleep; it just subsides into the subconscious state. And it is subconsciousness that makes continuity of consciousness possible during deep sleep. The theory of subconsciousness *(bhavaṅga-viññāṇa)* is important, not only for understanding the continuity of consciousness, but also for explaining *karma* and rebirth.

According to Nyanatiloka, "this so-called 'subconscious life-stream' or undercurrent of life is that by which might be explained the faculty of memory, paranormal psychic phenomena, mental and physical growth, *Karma* and Rebirth, etc."[76]

Now we shall consider how the theory of subconsciousness is related to the theories of *karma* and rebirth.

## REBIRTH OF CONSCIOUSNESS

Towards the end of the preceding chapter we remarked that one of the main problems for the Buddhist is to reconcile the doctrine of *anattā* with the beliefs in *karma* and rebirth. They have to answer this question: If there is no self, what is it that is reborn and experiences the results of *karma?* As T. W. Rhys Davids has pointed out: "We have thus arrived at a deadlock: to save what it holds to be a psychological truth Buddhism rejects the notion of a soul; to save what it holds to be the necessity of justice, it retains the belief in transmigration."[77] The word transmigration is misleading. The Buddhist doctrine of rebirth should be distinguished from the Upaniṣadic theory of a transmigrating self or soul. In Buddhism there is no permanent self which transmigrates from one life to another. In Buddhaghosa's words, "there is no entity, no self, no elements of being transmigrated from the last existence into the present one."[78]

If there is no transmigrating self, what is reborn into the next existence *(bhava)?* To this question, the Buddhist replies that *consciousness (viññāṇa) is reborn.* [79] In the *Mahānidāna-Sutta,* the Buddha says that were consciousness not to descend into the mother's womb, name-and-form of a new life would not come to birth.[80] Thus "the effective medium of rebirth is *viññāṇa*, consciousness."[81] Nevertheless this should not mislead us into thinking that it is one and the same consciousness that transmigrates from one existence to another. A monk called Sāti is said to have believed that one and the same consciousness is reborn into the next existence. Sāti, when asked by the Buddha to explain what he understands by consciousness, gives this answer: "It is this, Lord, that speaks, that feels, that experiences now here, now there, the function of deeds that are lovely and that are deprived."[82] It should be noted here that Sāti's definition of consciousness is similar to the Upaniṣadic definition of self *(ātman)*. He is, therefore, accused by the Buddha of distorting the Master's teaching. The Buddha says:

> *"But to whom, foolish man, do you understand the* dhamma *was taught by me thus? Has not consciousness generated by conditions been spoken of in many a figure by me, saying: Apart from condition there is no origination of consciousness?"*[83]

As mentioned earlier, consciousness is momentary; it never remains the same for any two consecutive moments. The stream of consciousness flows on because of the rapid succession of conscious moments. When one conscious act dies, another is born in its place, appropriating all the potentialities of the dying conscious act. In this way consciousness dies and is reborn every moment in our daily life. This explains why Buddhaghosa says that "the life of living beings lasts only for a single conscious moment."[84] The process of death and rebirth in daily life is applied to the dissolution of body and rebirth into the next life. Just as the present conscious moment is the result of the preceding conscious moment, so also the consciousness of a newborn child is the result of the consciousness of the dead man. The last moment of consciousness in the previous life is called "death-consciousness" *(cuti-citta)*, and the first moment of consciousness in the present life is called "rebirth-consciousness" (*paṭisandhi-citta*). "Immediately after that death-consciousness has ceased, a rebirth-consciousness arises and is established in the subsequent existence."[85] The rebirth-consciousness is called "*paṭisandhi*" because it links together two consecutive existences. And it is the death-consciousness that originates the rebirth-consciousness and is its immediate cause. At the moment of death, the death-consciousness in the preceding life perishes, immediately giving birth to the rebirth-consciousness in the succeeding life. It is to be understood here that the death-consciousness does not transmigrate from one life to another; it is only the cause of the appearance of the rebirth-consciousness in a new life. The two consciousnesses are neither the same nor different. As it is said in the Visuddhimagga: "Because the series is continuous, there is neither identity *(ekatā)* nor diversity *(nānatā)*."[86]

Death-consciousness and rebirth-consciousness are essentially of the nature of subconsciousness *(bhavaṅga-viññāṇa)*.[87] Thus Buddhaghosa says that the last subconsciousness in one existence is death consciousness and the first subconsciousness of another existence is rebirth consciousness.[88] The latter is followed upon by subconsciousness proper. Thereupon an innumerable series of subconsciousness flows on uninterruptedly, for as long as there is no processed consciousness to interfere with the course of the stream.[89]

## THE DOCTRINE OF KARMA

According to Buddhism, it is consciousness that is reborn. Its rebirth is due to the potentialities transmitted by the death-consciousness in the previous life. In the potentialities are included "*karma* that is enveloped by latent ignorance *(avijjānusaya)* and rooted in latent desire (*taṇhānusaya*)."[90] Therefore the rebirth-consciousness is conditioned by a past good or bad *karma* which predominates at the moment of death. The *karma* that conditions the rebirth-consciousness is called Reproductive *Karma* *(janaka-kamma)*.[91] Here we find a close relation between the Buddhist view on rebirth and the doctrine of *karma*. As Poussin has pointed out:

*"The doctrine of* karma *presupposes the belief in transmigration and is primarily a rationalistic and moral explanation of the variety of the conditions of living beings through many consecutive existences."*[92]

The theory of *karma* means all the speculations concerned with actions, and especially the belief in retribution of action. It is a theory of cause and effect, of action and reaction. According to this theory, action *(kamma)* produces its effect or result *(vipāka)*. A good action produces good effect and a bad action bad effect. As it is said in the *Saṁyutta-Nikāya:*

"According to the seed that's sown
So is the fruit ye reap therefrom.
The doer of good (will gather) good,
The doer of evil evil (reaps)."[93]

The Sanskrit word *'karma'*(Pali, *kamma)* literally means action or deed. But in Buddhism it means only 'intentional' or 'volitional' action, not all action. The Buddha, like Sartre, defines action or *karma* by intention or will *(cetanā):* "Intention, monks, is what I call action. Having intended, one performs action by body, speech or mind."[94] Here intention is all important. Action without intention is a mere happening. As it has not been intended or willed the action is as if it were not done. It will bear no fruit *(vipāka)*, for it is not accumulated or stored up *(upacita)*. According to Sartre, action, as intention, is a choice of an end. And the choice gives rise to the sense of responsibility. For the Buddhist, intentional or volitional action necessarily implies moral responsibility in the sense that the doer of action will experience its result. Man's present existence is said to be conditioned by his action in the past. The Buddha says: "Owners of their action are living beings, heirs to their action; action is the womb from which they are born, their action is their friend, their refuge."[95]

One may ask whether the theory of *karma* is compatible with the doctrine of *anattā*. If there is no self as an agent, what is it that performs action and accumulates and experiences the result of action? According to the Buddhist, intentional consciousness performs action. Consciousness also accumulates the result of action—"if a person even unknowingly performs a meritorious action, consciousness acquires merit."[96] When action produces result, it is consciousness that experiences it. But consciousness which performs action is not identical with consciousness which experiences the result. In fact, they are "neither the same nor different." To say that the doer of action and the experiencer of the result are absolutely the same is to hold the eternalistic view, and to say that the two are entirely different is to hold the annihilationistic view.[97] Avoiding the two extreme views, the Buddhist says that the doer of action and the experiencer of the result are neither the same nor different *(na ca so, na ca añño)*. We have already explained this when discussing the continuity of consciousness.[98]

Although *karma* is defined by intention, not all intentional action is called *karma*. The Buddha and *Arahant*s perform intentional action, but their action does not produce effect. It is a mere 'doing' *(kiriyā)* without result to be accumulated by consciousness. The Buddha and *Arahant*s do not accumulate fresh *karma* because they have eradicated greed *(lobha)*, hatred *(dosa)* and delusion *(moha)* which are regarded as the roots of *karma*. Hence action which is performed out of the threefold defilement produces result. "This action ripens whenever one is reborn, and wherever this action ripens, there one experiences the fruits of this action, be it in this life, or the next life, or in some future life."[99] Action which is done through the complete absence of greed, hatred and delusion does not produce result. Thus it is said:

> *"For the actions which are not done out of greed, hatred and delusion, which have not sprung from them, which have not their source or origin in them; such actions, through the absence of greed, hatred and delusion, are abandoned, rooted out, like a palm-tree torn out of the soil, destroyed, and not able to spring up again."*[100]

This statement clearly shows that the theory of *karma* cannot be regarded as a strict determinism (*niyatavāda*) because it does not state that every action must produce result. To say that all action produces result would be a wrong interpretation of the Buddhist theory of *karma*, for the Buddha says:

> *"If, monks, anyone says that a man must reap according to his actions, in that case, monks, there is no religious life, nor is any opportunity afforded for the entire extinction of suffering. But if any one says, monks, that the reward a man reaps accords with his actions, in that case, monks, there is a religious life, and opportunity is afforded for the entire extinction of suffering."* [101]

This is to say that the religious life would be futile unless man could change the course of *karma* by religious practice. If the human condition were the exclusive result of past actions, then present actions would all be predetermined and human effort, especially religious practice, would be fruitless.

## FREEDOM OF CONSCIOUSNESS

Now we can see that the Buddhist is not fatalist because he accepts the possibility of changing the result of *karma* by human effort. The present existence is not only the effect of past *karma* but also the active cause of existence in the future. Man's future depends on his action at the present. By his own effort, man can eradicate the roots of *karma*, and thereby prevent *karma* from ripening in the future. This efficacy of human effort implies a certain degree of human freedom. The evidence of freedom is from the fact that man feels free to act and exercise his effort, called 'initiative' (*ārabbhadhātu*), in various situations.[102] As is mentioned earlier, it is intention (*cetanā*) that the Buddha calls *karma*. This intention implies a choice, a selection of what to do. One may ask whether the choice is free. In other words, is intention or will (*cetanā*) in Buddhism free? Does the Buddhist share Sartre's view that consciousness is freedom? Before we answer these questions, it is necessary to find out what these thinkers mean by freedom.

As we have already seen, consciousness is viewed by Sartre

as free, partly because it is uncaused or spontaneous; that is, it is not generated by external causes. Consciousness is the cause of itself. The preceding consciousness, on passing away, does not give rise to its immediate successor. Sartre says: "Between two consciousnesses there is no cause and effect relationship ... One consciousness is not the cause of another."[103] Each consciousness, therefore, is not the consequence of antecedent causes; it is uncaused, original, spontaneous. Hence consciousness is free because it does not belong to the causal order of the world; it is nothingness.

If by freedom is meant "uncaused origination" or "spontaneity" as described above, then consciousness in Buddhism is not freedom. In Buddhism everything is "dependently originated" (*paṭiccasamuppanna*), nothing is uncaused. Even consciousness belongs to the causal order of the world. Each consciousness has causal relation with its predecessor. It is not self-caused or spontaneous. Thus consciousness and its psychic factors (*cetasika*) are not free. From this it follows that will or intention (*cetanā*), which is one of the psychic factors, *is not free in the sense of being spontaneous.*

But when Sartre talks of free choice of consciousness he contends that the choice is free if it is not determined by causes and motives. He then denies that causes and motives can determine man's choice.[104] Here Sartre uses the term freedom in the sense of "undetermined choice." And if by freedom we mean, not "uncaused origination," but rather "undetermined choice," then we can say that there is the notion of free choice in Buddhism. The choice is free if it is not determined by desire *(taṇhā)* which is regarded as the major motive of action The ordinary man *(puthujjana)* always has this motive; therefore he is not free. His freedom is present in inverse proportion to the motive; *the less desire he has, the more freedom he gains.* As it is said: "It is due to desire that man is bound and it is by surmounting desire that he is free. By the destruction of desire or craving all bonds are cut off."[105] The *Arahant*, therefore, has absolute freedom because he has eradicated desire. "Destroying desire at its root, free from hunger, one attains *Nirvāṇa*."[106] Here we find that in Buddhism the term freedom *(vimutti)* is a synonym for *Nirvāṇa*. As it is said in the *Saṁyutta-Nikāya*: "Freedom means Nirvāṇa."[107]

It should be noted here that in Buddhism the consciousness of the ordinary person (*puthujjana*) is not said to be inherently free, because it is under the influence of desires. To obtain freedom, consciousness must be purified of all desires. The entire process of purification is like a straight line between two points, namely, the point of consciousness with impurities and defilements *(kilesa)* at one end, and the point of consciousness with purity *(visuddhi)* at the other. In between the two there are gradual stages of purification of consciousness. Thus consciousness is classified into various levels in accordance with the degrees of freedom which it obtains. In Buddhism there are altogether four levels or spheres *(bhūmi)* of consciousness. They are *Kāmāvacara-citta* (consciousness pertaining to the sensuous sphere), *Rūpāvacara-citta* (consciousness pertaining to the form-sphere), *Arūpāvacara-citta* (consciousness pertaining to the formless sphere), and *Lokuttara-citta* (supramundane consciousness).[108]

## FOUR SPHERES OF CONSCIOUSNESS

1. *Kāmāvacara-citta* is consciousness which moves under the influence of desire. Consciousness of this level lacks freedom because it is influenced and controlled by desire. It is this desire, manifesting itself in the forms of various defilements, that gives rise to suffering. Hence this type of consciousness is subject to suffering, and it is regarded as consciousness of an ordinary person. The psychic factors which are the special contents of this type of consciousness are called hindrances *(nivaraṇa)*. They are sensuous desire *(kāmachanda)*, ill will *(vyāpāda)*, sloth and torpor *(thīna-middha)*, restlessness and anxiety *(uddhacca-kukkucca)*, and doubt *(vicikicchā)*. By practising concentration meditation (*samatha-bhāvanā*), one can purify consciousness of these hindrances and thereby attain consciousness of the second level.

2. *Rūpāvacara-citta* is consciousness arising from concentra-

tion on an object associated with form and color. It is in a state of trance *(jhāna)*. This type of consciousness has five psychic factors which are called the constituents of trance *(jhānaṅga)*. They are initial application *(vitakka)*, sustained application *(vicāra)*, rapture *(pīti)*, joy *(sukha)* and one-pointedness *(ekaggatā)*. By these five factors, the five hindrances are suppressed. There are five stages of trances. Reaching the fifth stage, consciousness is purified of major defilements. If directed rightly, it makes endeavor to develop subtle states of concentration on the formless objects and consequently move to the third level.

3. *Arūpāvacara-citta* is consciousness arising from concentration on formless objects. Its psychic factors are the same as those of consciousness which reaches the fifth stage of trance. Its objects, however, are different. It concentrates on formless objects such as infinite space, infinite consciousness and nothingness. Concentrating on these objects, consciousness possesses four stages of progress known as *Arūpa-samādhi*. With the attainment of the fourth stage, consciousness becomes immensely pure and subtle. All the major defiling factors are rendered functionless except the ten fetters (*saṁyojana*) existing as the seeds of defilements. Having attained full concentration, consciousness is ready to develop insight into the true nature of things by means of insight meditation *(vipassanā-bhāvanā)*. By this insight, the ten fetters are cut off and consciousness reaches the fourth and final level.

4. In contrast with the first three levels of consciousness which are mundane *(lokiya)*, *Lokuttara-citta* is supramundane *(lokuttara)*. The former are accumulating states whereas the latter is an eliminating one. In supramundane consciousness, the ten fetters are uprooted. They are personality belief (*sakkāya-diṭṭhi*), doubt *(vicikicchā)*, clinging to mere rules and rituals *(sīlabbata-parāmāsa)*, sensuous desire *(kāmarāga)*, ill-will *(vyāpāda)*, desire for fine-material existence *(rūpa-rāga)*, desire for immaterial existence *(arūpa-rāga)*, conceit (*māna*), restlessness (*uddhacca*), and ignorance *(avijjā)*. These ten fetters are not destroyed at one time. Their destruction varies in four stages of sainthood, namely, stream-winner *(sotāpanna)*, once returner (*sakadāgāmī*)

never-returner *(anāgāmī)* and liberated being *(arahanta)*. The liberated person or *Arahant* alone destroys all the fetters. The total destruction of the fetters, which are the last residue of defiling factors, liberates consciousness from all motives. Thus the consciousness of the *Arahant* obtains absolute freedom.

It is important to emphasize here that *the consciousness of the Arahant is free in the sense of being undetermined by motives*, not in the sense of spontaneity. His consciousness is still dependently originated. Each conscious moment is caused by the preceding moment. It is not self-caused or spontaneous. The idea of spontaneous consciousness is not acceptable to the Buddhist because it is incompatible with the law of Dependent Origination, according to which all things arise out of causes. That is why the Buddhist rejects the indeterministic *(adhicca-samuppanna)* theory which proposes that everything arises without cause or condition *(ahetu-appaccaya)*. The Buddhist theory of Dependent Origination is the middle path. It "stands midway between Indeterminism (*adhicca-samuppanna*) and the Strict Determinism of *niyatavāda*."[109]

## TEMPORALITY

Arising out of causes and conditions, consciousness is a conditioned thing *(saṅkhata-dhamma)*. Since all conditioned things are impermanent, consciousness is also impermanent. To say that consciousness is impermanent is to say that it is temporal *(kālika)*. Here the term temporality is used to connote the fact of change as well as the subjective experience of temporal continuity.[110] According to the Buddhist, not only is consciousness momentary, but also the material object, which changes every moment. Unlike Sartre, the Buddhist thinks that impermanence is the characteristic of the material object. It is impermanent, and hence temporal.

The Buddhist does not regard time *(kāla)* as an all-pervading principle which governs everything. Universal time is a mere concept *(paññatti)* and has no objective existence. "Time is eventuation or happening, there being no such thing as time exempt from events."[111] Thus we cannot be aware of time apart from the succession of events. In the *Kathāvatthu* it is said that the division of time into past, present, and future is only conventional without any basis of reality; there is no ontological basis for the time-distinctions.[112] The past and the future have no existence since "what is past is got rid of and the future has not come."[113] Only the present has existence. If we grant existence to the past and the future then we have to admit that a thing has existence all the time, i.e. its existence is extended to both the past and the future. This would amount to admitting that the thing is eternal. Such a position would be inconsistent with the Buddha's statement that "impermanent are all conditioned things; their nature is to arise and perish."[114]

Hence the Buddhist would say that the present *is*. This is opposed to Sartre's statement that the present *is not*.[115] For the Buddhist, the present exists, not in the sense of Sartre's being-in-itself, but in the sense of becoming (*bhava*). For the Buddhist, the present alone is real, the past and the future are unreal. As it is said: "Now only the present existence is real, unreal the past and the future existence."[116] Thus the *Arahant* lives fully in the present.[117]

It is necessary to mention here that by the term "present" (*paccuppanna*) we mean the "momentary present" (*khaṇapaccuppanna*). The moment of consciousness "which reaches genesis, development and dissolution is the momentary present."[118] Each conscious moment, as we saw, is extremely short. And the life-moment of living beings is as short as a single moment of their consciousness. It is said in the Visuddhimagga:

> *"Just as a chariot wheel, when it is rolling, rolls only on one point of (the circumference of) its tyre, and, when it is at rest, rests only on one point, so too the life of living beings lasts only for a single conscious moment. When that consciousness has ceased, the being is said to have ceased, as it is said: 'in a past conscious moment "he did live," not "he does live," not "he will live." In a future conscious moment, not "he did live," not "he does live," but "he will live." In the present*

*conscious moment, not "he did live," but "he does live," not "he will live".'"*[119]

Although the present conscious moment alone exists, the rapid succession of conscious moments gives rise to the reflective experience of temporal continuity. The moments do not have "distinct existence," for each of them is conditioned by its immediate successor. They are not completely separated from each other. They appear to be discrete only when we analyze them by logical analysis. Otherwise they constitute a continuous stream. "Each momentary state or uprising of mind (*ekakkhaṇika-cittuppāda*) is logically complex and analyzable, but psychologically, actually, a simple indivisible process."[120] We have already seen that each conscious moment is by nature related to its predecessor and successor. The present moment of consciousness is a 'whole' consisting of three submoments, namely, genesis, development, and dissolution. The genesis is the submoment when the present consciousness arises out of the karma-energy transmitted by the past consciousness. This is the point which connects the present with the past. The dissolution is the submoment when the present consciousness, on passing away, transmits its karma-energy to the future consciousness. And this is the point which connects the present with the future. In this way, conscious moments succeed one another. And the reflective experience of temporal continuity is due to the reflection upon the rapid succession of conscious moments. "They present a continuous spectrum of consciousness in which one state shades off into another, laterally and lineally, so that it is hard to say where or when one ends and another begins."[121]

## THE CONCEPT OF NIRVĀṆA

From the foregoing discussion it is clear that the present is not cut off from the past and the future. The present exists as the effect of the past and as the cause of the future. The present, as a 'whole' consisting of three submoments, has to be its past and future, not in the mode of identity, but in the mode of "neither identity nor diversity." The temporal continuity flows on till *Nirvāṇa* is realized, as the consciousness of one who has attained *Nirvāṇa* is not reborn.[122] Consciousness in Buddhism is not always a "useless passion." There is time when passion or desire is eliminated from consciousness and thereby ceases to be the cause of suffering. Desire is destroyed when *Nirvāṇa* is realized. The Buddha says: "The extinction of desire is *Nirvāṇa*."[123] Again, "he who destroys desire overcomes all suffering."[124] Desire is not an inherent component of consciousness; it is one of the psychic factors. Desire, according to the law of Dependent Origination, is conditioned by feeling (*vedanā*), and this feeling is threefold—pleasant, unpleasant and indifferent, which respectively tend to produce greed, hatred and delusion. As it is pointed out in the Majjhima-Nikāya: "Friend Visākha, a tendency to greed lies latent in pleasant feeling, a tendency to repugnance lies latent in unpleasant feeling, a tendency to delusion lies latent in indifferent feeling."[125] Thus we can say that greed, hatred and delusion are three forms in which desire manifests itself. This explains why at times *Nirvāṇa* is described in terms of the destruction of the threefold defilement: "That which is the destruction of greed, hatred and delusion is called *Nirvāṇa*."[126] When consciousness is freed from greed, hatred and delusion, which are the roots of *karma*, consciousness becomes "karmically inoperative" (*kiriyā-citta*). It no longer accumulates fresh karma-energy. And consciousness whose karma-energy is exhausted will not be reborn after death. When an *Arahant* dies, his "body is broken, perception is stopped, all feelings are cooled, mental formations are calmed down, *consciousness has come to an end*."[127] His consciousness is not reborn because the cause of its rebirth has been destroyed. "Through the cessation of ignorance, *karma*-formations cease; through the cessation of *karma*-formations, consciousness ceases; through the cessation of consciousness, name-and-form ceases ..."[128] Since consciousness is the effective medium of rebirth, the cessation of consciousness is the cessation of *Saṁsāra*, i.e. the series of rebirths. *Nirvāṇa*, therefore, is said to be "the cessation of existence" (*bhavànirodha*).[129] Having attained *Nirvāṇa*, the *Ara-*

*hant* knows that "finished is birth, lived is the religious life, what should be done is done, nothing more is left to be done."[130]

Now one question arises: If consciousness is not-self, then who realizes *Nirvāṇa*? We have shown earlier that there is no self as thinker behind the thought, it is the thought that thinks. In like manner, there is no self behind the realization of *Nirvāṇa;* it is wisdom (*paññā*) that realizes *Nirvāṇa*. When wisdom, which is one of the psychic factors, is developed by means of insight meditation it sees the reality of things. When the reality is seen, the concept of the phenomenal world (*papañca*) is destroyed.[131] Ignorance (*avijjā*) is eradicated and in its place arises wisdom. Then all forces which produce the series of rebirths in ignorance become calmed and are unable to generate any more *karma*-energy, because there is no more illusion, no more desire for existence. As such, *Nirvāṇa* is regarded as the realization of things as they are. It is just a change of our attitude towards things. The change follows the elimination of ignorance which is responsible for the appearance of the phenomenal world: "Not constituting, not thinking out for being or for nonbeing, he grasps after nothing in the world; not grasping, he is not troubled; being untroubled, he himself attains *Nirvāṇa*."[132]

It is interesting to note that this conception of *Nirvāṇa* as the realization of the true nature of things has been developed in Mahāyāna Buddhism. According to Nagarjuna, "things" are phenomena or *Saṁsāra*, and their "true nature" is *Nirvāṇa*. In essence *Saṁsāra* is not different from *Nirvāṇa*. Nagarjuna writes: "*Saṁsāra* has no difference whatever from *Nirvāṇa* and *Nirvāṇa* has no difference whatever from *Saṁsāra*."[133] Hence the reality is one; it becomes different on the basis of our viewpoint. *Nirvāṇa* when looked at from the standpoint of thought-construction (*vikalpa*) is the phenomenal world; and phenomena devoid of superimposed thought-construction (*nirvikalpa*) are *Nirvāṇa*. The difference between the two is *epistemic*, and *not ontological.*[134] According to Nagarjuna, *Nirvāṇa* is the Absolute Reality or Ultimate Truth (*paramartha-satya*) whereas the phenomenal world is the Conventional Truth (*samvrti-satya*). We find, in early Buddhism, the germ of Nagarjuna's two-truth theory in the *Majjhima-Nikāya*, where it is said:

> *"Assured is freedom* (vimutti) *which rests on Truth. Monk, that which is unreality* (mosadhamma) *is false; that which is reality,* Nirvāṇa, *is Truth* (sacca). *Therefore, monk, a person so endowed is endowed with this Ultimate Truth. For the Ultimate Noble Truth* (paramaṁ ariyasaccaṁ) *is* Nirvāṇa, *which is reality."*[135]

## THE ONTOLOGICAL STATUS OF NIRVĀṆA

Since *Nirvāṇa* is regarded as the "cessation of existence" *(bhavanirodha)*[136] or the end of *Saṁsāra*, it is viewed as annihilation by some thinkers. The Buddha himself was accused of preaching annihilation. To clarify his position, the Buddha says:

> *"In this respect one may rightly say of me that I teach annihilation, that I propound my doctrine for the purpose of annihilation, and that I herein train my disciples: for certainly I do teach annihilation—the annihilation, namely, of greed, hatred and delusion, as well as of the manifold evil and unwholesome things."*[137]

What we can say here is that *Nirvāṇa* is not self-annihilation, for there is no self to annihilate. If at all, it is the annihilation of the ignorance *(avijjā)*, of the false idea of self.

Followers of the Buddha, however, hold different views on the ontological status of *Nirvāṇa*. The Sautrantika, for example, contends that *Nirvāṇa* does not have a positive reality; it is nothingness *(abhāva)*. Just as space *(ākāśa)* is the absence of a solid body or anything tangible, so also *Nirvāṇa* is the absence of causes that are responsible for rebirth. The Sautrantika's position appears to be nihilistic.[138] Unlike the Sautrantika, the Vijñāṇavādin maintains that *Nirvāṇa* has a positive reality. The realization of *Nirvāṇa* eliminates the unreality of the phenomenal world. What remains after the realization is Store-consciousness or *Ālayavijñāṇa*. The Store-consciousness is the absolute, the ultimate source of the phenomenal world. The realization of *Nirvāṇa* is nothing but the rediscovery of the Store-consciousness. "*Nirvāṇa* is the *Ālayavijñāṇa* where a revulsion takes place by *self-realization*."[139] Here the conception of *Nirvāṇa* as self-realization is analogous to the Upaniṣadic conception of *Mokṣa* as the realization of *ātman*.

Rejecting the nihilistic conception of *Nirvāṇa*, the early Buddhist maintains that *Nirvāṇa* is not a nonexistence. That is, *Nirvāṇa* is *not* annihilation, though no Store-consciousness remains in the state of *Nirvāṇa*. The *Abhidhamma* considers *Nirvāṇa* to be a transcendental entity, independently existent. The *Kathāvatthu* conceives *Nirvāṇa* as an external, unchangeable state which exists by itself.[140] In the *Visuddhimagga*, Buddhaghosa rejects the view that *Nirvāṇa* is nonexistent. According to him, the mere fact that *Nirvāṇa* is not apprehended by an ordinary man does not prove that *Nirvāṇa* does not exist. "That is not so, because it is apprehensible by the (right) means. For it is apprehensible by some, by the right means, in other words, by the way that is appropriate to it (the way of virtue, concentration and wisdom) ..."[141] *Nirvāṇa* is so subtle that a Noble One's eye *(ariya-cakkhu)* alone can see it.[142] *Nirvāṇa* is uncreated and hence free from ageing and death. And it is because of the absence of its creation, ageing and death that *Nirvāṇa* is permanent *(nicca)*. Thus *Nirvāṇa* is not a nonexistence; rather it is positive, permanent reality. To substantiate his view, Buddhaghosa quotes the Buddha's words from the *Udāna:*

> *"Monks, there is an unborn, an unbecome, an unmade, an unconditioned. If that unborn, unbecome, unmade, unconditioned were not, an escape from what is born, become, made, conditioned would not be apparent. But since, monks, there is an unborn, unbecome, unmade, unconditioned, therefore, the escape from what is born, become, made, conditioned is apparent."*[143]

The Commentary of the *Visuddhimagga* explains that, with these statements from the *Udāna*, the Buddha proclaims the actual existence of *Nirvāṇa* in the ultimate sense. If the unconditioned, i.e. *Nirvāṇa*, were nonexistent, then no escape from the conditioned, i.e. the five aggregates, would be possible.[144]

Thus *Nirvāṇa* as conceived in early Buddhism is not nonexistence or utter annihilation. It is the realm of being which transcends the phenomenal world (*lokuttara*). *Nirvāṇa* is the unconditioned (*asaṅkhata*), as opposed to the conditioned (*saṅkhata*), i.e. phenomena. Negative terms like "unconditioned" and "uncreated" do not connote nonexistence. *Nirvāṇa* is described in negative terms because it cannot be described in positive terms. *Nirvāṇa* is indescribable and uncharacterizable. It is not like anything we find in our experience of the phenomenal world. In order to describe the nature of *Nirvāṇa*, the Buddha had to use negative statements like the following:

> *"Monks, there exists the sphere wherein is neither earth nor water nor fire nor air; wherein is neither the sphere of infinite space nor of infinite consciousness nor of nothingness nor of neither-perception-nor-non-perception; where there is neither this world nor a world beyond nor moon-and-sun; this, monks, I say, is no coming and going; there is no duration, no falling, nor arising. There is neither foothold nor development nor any basis. That indeed is the end of suffering."*[145]

As we saw, negative statements like "*neti, neti*" (not this, not this) were employed by the Upaniṣadic thinkers to describe the reality of *ātman*.

## UNDETERMINED QUESTIONS

Not only is the reality of *Nirvāṇa* indescribable but also the destiny of the liberated person. The question as to whether the person who has attained *Nirvāṇa* continues to exist after death cannot be answered either positively or negatively. Such a question belongs to the group of ten questions known as undetermined questions (*avyākata-pañhā*). There are four undetermined questions about the destiny of the liberated person:

1. The liberated one (*Tathāgata*) exists after death.
2. The liberated one does not exist after death.
3. The liberated one exists and does not exist after death.

4. The liberated one neither exists nor does not exist after death.[146]

The Buddha gave no specific answer to any of these questions. One of the reasons for the 'silence' of the Buddha is that the phrases 'exists,' 'does not exist,' etc., are misleading because they have a spatiotemporal connotation and hence are inapplicable to *Nirvāṇa* which is beyond space and time and cannot be located (*na katthaci, na kuhiñci*). It, therefore, escapes the conceptual framework necessary for our expression in languages. The mystery of the liberated person lies in the fact that he is no longer identified with any of the five aggregates by which the ordinary person is known. The descriptions of his destiny in terms of the four alternatives mentioned above are out of place. That explains why it is said in the Sutta-Nipāta: "The person who has attained the goal is beyond measure (*na pamānaṁ atthi*); he does not have that with which one can speak of him."[147] Seeing that nothing can be spoken about the destiny of the liberated person, the Buddha keeps silent. The Buddha's approach, in this respect, is similar to that of Wittgenstein who ends his Tractatus with this famous statement: *"What we cannot speak about we must pass over in silence."*[148]

## A SUMMARY

So far the Buddhist conception of consciousness has been discussed in some detail. We shall now summarize what we have discovered in the course of the discussions.

Consciousness is without self or ego. It is defined by *intentionality;* that is, consciousness is consciousness of something. When consciousness is aware of an object, it is not aware of itself; this is to say that consciousness is *not* self-conscious or self-transparent. Devoid of the self, consciousness is non-substantial and impermanent. It arises and perishes every moment. Thus consciousness is *momentary* or instantaneous. Each moment of consciousness is subdivided into three instants, namely, genesis, development and dissolution. Every conscious moment is not being-in-itself; it does not have a "distinct existence." It is a becoming (*bhava*). Consciousness is by nature dependently originated; hence it is not spontaneous or self-caused. Moments of consciousness are causally related by way of contiguity, immediacy, absence and disappearance. The past moment of consciousness, on passing away, transmits all its contents to the present moment. Thus the present conscious moment was born an owner of the contents, including *karma*-energy, of its predecessor. The past and the present moments of consciousness are *neither the same nor different*. Causal relations, therefore, effect the unity and continuity of consciousness. The rapid succession of conscious moments constitutes the stream of consciousness. The subjective experience of temporal continuity arises out of reflection upon fleeting conscious moments. The stream of consciousness flows on without interruption. When man is in deep, dreamless sleep, his consciousness subsides into the subconscious state or *bhavaṅga*. It is this *bhavaṅga-viññāṇa* or subconsciousness that accumulates the results of *karma* and is reborn after death. The sequence of rebirths or *Saṁsāra* is cut off when consciousness realizes *Nirvāṇa*. Before realizing *Nirvāṇa*, consciousness is not free because its intention (*cetanā*) is determined by desire (*taṇhā*). It is free when desire is eradicated in the state of *Nirvāṇa*. Thus consciousness is not a "useless passion." When an *Arahant* dies, his consciousness is not reborn; therefore, *Nirvāṇa* is the cessation of *Saṁsāric* existence (*bhavanirodha*).

## SUÑÑATĀ AND NOTHINGNESS

From this summary it is clear that consciousness in Buddhism is not nothingness (*natthitā*). Its egolessness does not imply nothingness. In spite of being emptied of the substantial ego, consciousness is not contentless. Consciousness has *something* as its contents. Feeling (*vedanā*), perception (*saññā*) and mental formations (*saṅkhāra*) are contents of consciousness. Arising and perishing together with consciousness, they are called *cetasika* or psychic factors. Consciousness in its purest form does not arise in utter separation from *cetasika*; it is always accompanied by some factors. Even the *Arahant*'s consciousness is not devoid of psychic factors. At his death consciousness and its factors disappear together. That explains why when an *Arahant* called Dabba Mallaputta died, it was said that his "body is broken, perception is stopped, all feelings are cooled, mental formations are calmed down, consciousness has come to an end."[149]

Furthermore, consciousness cannot be regarded as nothingness for the reason that *it is what it is* at the present moment. Consciousness, as we saw, is not self-conscious. When it is aware of an object, it is not implicitly aware of itself as not being that object; that is, at that very moment, consciousness is. Being unself-conscious, consciousness is not able to tear itself away from its object. Nor can it withdraw itself from the causal order of *Saṁsāra*. Consciousness is a part of the causal process as indicated in the law of Dependent Origination: "Conditioned by ignorance are *karma*-formations; conditioned by *karma*-formations is consciousness; conditioned by consciousness is name-and-form ..."[150] When *Nirvāṇa* is realized, the causes of rebirth of consciousness are destroyed and consciousness comes to an end at the death of the *Arahant*. This indicates that consciousness is not nothingness, for if consciousness were nothingness it would be meaningless to talk of its end.

It is said that consciousness is 'void' or 'empty' (*suñña*).[151] Here emptiness (*suññatā*) of consciousness should not be understood in the sense of nothingness, for the term *'suñña'* is used as a synonym for *'anattā.'* Thus consciousness is empty because it is *"empty of a self and anything belonging to a self."*[152] It may be added here that even the concept of 'emptiness' (Sanskrit, *śūnyatā)* in Mahāyāna Buddhism does not refer to nothingness in the Sartrean sense. The terms *'śūnya'* (empty) and *'śūnyatā'* (emptiness) are applied to both the phenomenal world and *Nirvāṇa*. Phenomena are *śūnya* as they are empty of thing-hood *(nihsvabhāva);* for they are dependent on each other (*pratītya-samutpanna*). As Nagarjuna has pointed out: "Since there is no element *(dharma)* which comes into existence without conditions, there is no element which is not *'śūnya'*."[153] In this sense *śūnyatā* simply means conditionality of all phenomena. It is a synonym for *Pratītyasamutpāda* or the Principle of Dependent Origination.[154] In this sense, *śūnyatā* is not nothingness.

> *"Therefore, 'emptiness,' according to the Buddhists, signifies negatively the absence of particularity, the nonexistence of individuals as such, and positively the ever-changing state of the phenomenal world, a constant flux of becoming, an eternal series of causes and effects. It must not be understood in the sense of annihilation or absolute nothingness."*[155]

The term *'śūnyatā'* is also applied to the Absolute or *Nirvāṇa*, "though in different sense."[156] The Absolute is *śūnya* as it is utterly devoid of the conceptual distinctions of existence and nonexistence, free from all subjectivity *(nirvikaḷpa, nisprapañca)*. Hence both affirmative predicates *(sat, bhāva)* and negative predicates *(asat, abhāva)* are equally denied of the Absolute. This absence of predicates, however, only shows that the Absolute is indescribable, not that it is a lack of Being. As T.R.V. Murti has pointed out:

> *"We are expressly warned not to take* śūnyatā *as* abhāvadṛsti *(Negation).* Tattava *(the Real) is accepted explicitly; but we are forbidden to characterize and clothe it in empirical terms ... The Absolute is taken as the reality of things* (dharmānaṁ dharmatā)*, as their true nature* (bhūta-koti) *and suchness* (tathatā)*. It is identified with the Perfect Being*—Tathāgata.*"*[157]

Thus 'emptiness' (Pali, *suññatā;* Sanskrit, *śūnyatā)* in Buddhism does not signify nothingness, at least in the Sartrean sense of the term. Consciousness is said to be empty because it is devoid of a self and anything belonging to a self, not because it is lack of being. Hence consciousness in Buddhism is not nothingness. In this respect, the Buddhist conception of consciousness is different from the Sartrean conception of consciousness as nothingness. In the next chapter, we shall compare these two conceptions of consciousness and try to find out how they are similar to, and different from, each other.

## NOTES

1 C. A. F. Rhys Davids, *Introduction to Buddhist Psychology (Dhammasaṅganī)*, Oriental Books Reprint Co., 1975, p. LX.
2 Vism. XVIII , 590.
3 Tiwary, M., "Pari-Nibbāna", in *Bobhi-Raśmi,* ed. by M. Tiwary, First International Conference on Buddhism and National Cultures, New Delhi, 1984, p. 92.
4 D. III. 103; S. XII. 61.
5 Abhs. I. 1.
6 Dhs. Section 1191.
7 Abhs. II. 1.
8 Abhs. II. 2.
9 Abhs. VIII. 9.
10 DhsA. 63 : *"Ārammaṇaṁ cintetīti cittaṁ".*
11 Miln. 62; DhsA., 112.
12 M.I. III. *"Tinnaṁ saṅgati phasso".*
13 Stcherbatsky, Th., *Buddhist Logic,* Vol. 1, Dover Publications, 1962, p. 166.
14 Kvu. XVI. 4.
15 Kvu. A. quoted in S.Z. Aung and Mrs. Rhys Davids, *Points of Controversy,* PTS, 1915, p. 305.
16 Ibid.
17 Ibid., p. 183.
18 Nyāyabindu, I, 10, p. 11.
19 Candrakirti, Mādhyamikakārikā-vṛtti, (Prasannapāda), p. 61.
20 Ledi Sayadaw, *The Manuals of Buddhism,* Mahamakut Press, Bangkok, 1978, p. 67.
21 Vism. XV. 488-489.
22 Jayatilleke, K. N., *The Contemporary Relevance of Buddhist Philosophy,* BPS, 1969, p. 15.
23 S. XXII. 79; Vism. XVIII. 587.
24 Vism. XVIII. 587.
25 M. I. 298.
26 M. I. 111.
27 Nyanatiloka, *Buddhist Dictionary,* BPS, 1972, p. 123.
28 Dhp. 254.
29 Ud. 8.
30 SN. 1119.
31 A. II. 48.
32 AA. I. 95.
33 AA. I. 94; Cf. K. N. Jayatilleke, *Early Buddhist Theory of Knowledge,* pp. 361-368.
34 A. I. 10.
35 S. XII. 61.
36 DhsA. 420; Abhs. IV. 3.
37 Aung., S.Z., *Introduction to Compendium of Philosophy,* PTS., 1956, p. 26.

38 D. III. 105.
39 Abhs. V. 15.
40 Cf. the famous statement of Heraclitus: "You cannot step twice into the same river, for fresh waters are ever flowing in upon you."
41 Abhs. VIII. 9.
42 Aung, S. Z. , op. cit., p. 42.
43 Miln., p. 40.
44 Johansson, R., *The Psychology of Nirvāna*, George Allen and Unwin, 1969, p. 71.
45 Aung, S. Z., op. cit., p. 42.
46 Ayer, A. J., *The Problem of Knowledge*, Penguin Books, 1976, pp. 198-199.
47 Ibid., p. 195.
48 Ibid., p. 199.
49 Hume, D., *A Treatise of Human Nature*, Oxford, 1975, p. 636.
50 BN. 190.
51 D. II. 55.
52 S. XII. 20.
53 A.V. 2, 3, 312.
54 Jayatilleke, K.N., *Early Buddhist Theory of Knowledge*, p. 448.
55 M. I. 257.
56 James, W., *The Principles of Psychology*, Vol, 1, Dover Publications, 1950, p. 239.
57 Ibid., pp. 342-350.
58 Ibid., p. 344.
59 Ibid., p. 338.
60 Ibid.
61 Ibid.
62 Abhs. V. 15.
63 Radhakrishnan, S., *Indian Philosophy*, Vol. 1, 1983, p. 258.
64 Miln. 299.
65 Aung. S. Z., *Compendium of Philosophy*, pp. 265-266
66 Ibid., p. 266.
67 Ibid.
68 Narada, *A Manual of Abhidhamma*, BPS., 1975, p. 211.
69 Abhs. IV. 3.
70 Ibid.
71 Ibid.
72 Malalasekera, G. P., (ed.), *Encyclopedia of Buddhism*, vol. 111, 1971, p. 17.
73 Vism. XIX. 600.
74 Rao, K. R., "Early Buddhistic Psychology of Transcendence," paper presented at the First International Conference on Buddhism and National Cultures, New Delhi, 1984, p. 4.
75 Narada, op. cit., p. 164.
76 Nyanatiloka, op. cit., p. 33.
77 T. W. Rhys Davids, "On Nirvāna, and on Buddhist Doctrines of the Group, the Saṅkhāras, Karma and the Paths", *The Contemporary Review*, XXIX, 1877, p. 249.

78 Vism. XVII, 553-4.
79 Vism. XVII, 554; Abhs. V. 12.
80 D. II. 63.
81 Johansson, R., op. cit., p 39.
82 M. I. 258.
83 Ibid.
84 Vism. VIII. 238.
85 Abhs. V. 12.
86 Vism. XVIII. 554.
87 Aung, S. Z., op. cit., p. 267.
88 Vism. XIV. 460.
89 Vism. XIV. 458; Abhs. V. 15.
90 Abhs. V. 12.
91 Vism. XIX. 601.
92 Poussin, Louis La Vallee, *The Way to Nirvana*, Sri Satguru Publications, 1982, p. 58.
93 S. XI. 1. 10.
94 A. V.I. 63.
95 M. III. 203.
96 S. XII. 6.51.
97 S. XII. 2.18.
98 See above,. pp. 141-5.
99 A. III. 33.
100 A. III. 33.
101 A. III. 99.
102 A. III. 337-8.
103 Sartre, J-P., *The Psychology of Imagination*, Methuen & Co. Ltd., London, 1972, p. 27.
104 See above pp. 69-70.
105 S. I. 7.9.
106 S. XXII. 22.
107 S. XXIII. 1 : "Vimutti … nibbānatthā".
108 Abhs. I. 2.
109 Jayatilleke, K. N. op. cit., p. 445.
110 Sinha, B. M., *Time and Temporality in Samkhya-Yoga and Abhidharma Buddhism*, Munshiram, 1983, p. 11.
111 Abhidhānappadipikā-Sūci, quoted in Points of Controversy, p. 392.
112 Kvu. I. 6. 5.
113 M. III. 187.
114 S.I. 1.
115 See above. p. 63.
116 D. I. 201.
117 S. I. 1.10.
118 DhsA. 420.
119 Vism. VIII. 238.
120 Aung, S. Z., *Points of Controversy*, p. 393.
121 Ibid.

122 S.N. 734.
123 S. XXIII. 2.
124 Dhp. 354.
125 M.I. 303.
126 S. XXXVIII. 1.
127 Ud. 93.
128 M. III. 68.
129 S. XII. 68.
130 M. III. 224.
131 See above, pp 132-3.
132 M. III. 244.
133 MK. XXV. 19.
134 Murti, T. R. V., *The Central Philosophy of Buddhism*, 1980, p. 141.
135 M. III. 245.
136 S. XII. 68.
137 A. III. 12.
138 Cf. Chandrakaew, C., *Nibbāna*, Mahachula Buddhist University, Bangkok, 1982; pp. 95-97.
139 Laṅkāvatāra Sutra, p. 62.
140 Kvu. I. 6.8.
141 Vism. XVI. 508.
142 Cf. M.I. 510.
143 Ud. 80-81.
144 Paramattha-mañjusā. Pali-Thai, vol. VI, Bhumibalo Bhikkhu Foundation, 1990, p. 113.
145 Ud. 80.
146 Cūla-Māluṅkaya Sutta, M. I. 427; Aggi-Vacchagotta Sutta, M.I. 484.
147 Sutta-Nipāta, verse 1076.
148 Wittgenstein, L., *Tractatus Logico-philosophicus*, tr. by D. F. Pears and B. F. McGuinness, Routledge and Kegan Paul, 1961, 6. 54.
149 Ud. 93.
150 M. III. 163-4.
151 Paṭisambhidāmagga, Vol. II, p. 177; S. XXXV. 85.
152 Ibid.
153 MK. XXIV. 19.
154 MK. XXIV. 18. *"Yah Pratītyasamutpādah śūnyatām tām pracaksamahe"*
155 Suzuki, D. T., *Outlines of Mahāyāna Buddhism*, 1963, p. 173.
156 Radhakrishnan, S., op. cit., p. 702.
157 Murti, T. R. V., op. cit., pp. 312-313.

# PART THREE

# REFLECTIONS AND COMPARISONS

# V

# REFLECTIONS AND COMPARISONS

In the preceding four chapters we have followed the course of Sartre's and the Buddhist's thought in detail in an effort to understand their non-egological treatments of consciousness. We have remarked, in passing, some points of similarity and difference. In this chapter we shall reflect upon what has already been discussed and, in the light of those discussions, compare and contrast Sartre's treatment of consciousness with that of the Buddhist.

At first glance we find that Sartre's and the Buddhist's treatments of consciousness are similar in that they are characterized as *non-egological*. In formulating their own theories of consciousness, Sartre and the Buddhist alike have attacked the *egology* or *attavāda* propounded by their predecessors and contemporaries. Sartre thus rejects Husserl's doctrine of the transcendental ego whereas the Buddhist repudiates the *ātman* theory, the chief proponents of which are the Upaniṣadic thinkers. The outcome of their attack is much the same; they reach the conclusion that *there is no permanent self or ego within or behind the stream of consciousness;* that is, consciousness is egoless or not-self *(anattā).* This is a basic view shared by Sartre and the Buddhist.

## ĀTMAN AND THE TRANSCENDENTAL EGO

We have shown in Chapter III that the Husserlian ego is not quite the same as the Upaniṣadic *ātman.*[1] It may be added here that the difference is due to the fact that the former is established on epistemological grounds whereas the latter is founded on metaphysical and ethical grounds. As we saw, the transcendental ego is introduced by Husserl for the purpose of unifying the stream of experience, it is the subject-pole of experience. In this sense the ego may be regarded as the *epistemological self.* The Upaniṣadic *ātman,* on the other hand, is conceived as a permanent entity underlying the ever-changing mental phenomena; it is the substance of the person. In this respect, *ātman is known as the metaphysical self.* Apart from this, the existence of *ātman* is presupposed in order to give a justification for the pursuit of *Mokṣa* or self-realization. On this ethical ground, *ātman is* endowed with immortality and identity with the ultimate reality or *Brahman.* Husserl's transcendental ego is different from *ātman* mainly because it *lacks* immortality and identity with ultimate reality. Nevertheless the transcendental ego and *ātman* are *analogous* in that they refer to *something permanent residing in the stream of ever-changing conscious acts.* And this permanent thing in consciousness—be it called transcendental ego or *ātman*—is rejected by Sartre and the Buddhist.

## PURPOSES IN REJECTING THE SELF

Sartre and the Buddhist have different purposes in rejecting the permanent self. Sartre's interest in denying the transcendental ego is purely theoretical in that his aim, as pronounced in *The*

*Transcendence of the Ego,* is to purge phenomenology of idealism. Sartre believes that phenomenology is realistic but it is reproached for being an idealism owing to Husserl's doctrine of the transcendental ego. To defend phenomenology against this reproach, Sartre finds it necessary to reject the transcendental ego. In *Being and Nothingness* Sartre repudiates the ego because he wants to establish his phenomenological ontology. Sartre's ontology can stand only when the transcendental ego is rejected; that is, when all being is on the side of the object and the egoless consciousness is nothingness. Hence Sartre's rejection of the transcendental ego is a prerequisite of the possibility of his phenomenological ontology.

The Buddhist's theoretical aim in rejecting the self theory is to dissociate himself from the two extreme views, namely, annihilationism *(ucchedavāda)* and eternalism *(sassatavāda)* which in his view are both defined in one way or another by the self theory. Those who believe in the existence of the self have to admit that it is perishable or imperishable. For the annihilationist the self is perishable whereas for the eternalist it is imperishable. The Buddhist regards the two views as 'wrong views' (*micchādiṭṭhi*). The Buddhist is neither annihilationist nor eternalist because he believes that there is no self to annihilate or persist. He claims that "all *dhammas* are not-self" *(sabbe dhammā anattā).* With this statement the Buddhist rejects the Upaniṣadic thinkers' substance view of the world, maintaining that nothing exists in itself for everything is dependently originated *(paṭiccasamuppanna).* Thus the important theory of Dependent Origination (*paṭiccasamuppāda*) can stand only when the self theory is rejected.

Moreover, unlike Sartre, the Buddhist has a practical purpose in rejecting the self theory. Like the other teachings of the Buddha, the *anattā* doctrine has *Nirvāṇa* or the cessation of suffering as its purpose.[2] The idea of self is considered as the manifestation of the grasping called *attavādupādāna*. This grasping is similar to what the Western psychologists call "self-love."[3] The Buddhist thinks that the grasping of the self is the main origin of suffering. To bring suffering to an end, one has to get rid of its cause, i.e. the grasping of the self. So long as the grasping persists, there can be no complete cessation of suffering. Thus the practical purpose of the Buddhist's doctrine of *anattā* is to enable one to shed the grasping of the self.

## THE EMPIRICAL SELF

Here one question arises: If the five aggregates are by nature not-self as the Buddhist claims, whence does the idea of the self come? What is this self which is the object of grasping *(upādāna)?* The Buddhist's answer is that the idea of the self is a mental construct produced by unwise attention *(ayoniso-manasikāra).* This constituted self is the object of grasping. Since the grasping of the self gives rise to suffering, one has to get rid of the idea of the self. This practical bearing is not found in Sartre's challenge to Husserl's egology.

Although Sartre rejects the transcendental ego, he admits that there is an empirical ego constituted or 'made-to-be' by impure reflection. Here we find another similarity in Sartre's and the Buddhist's treatments of consciousness. *Both of them reject the permanent ego and yet accept the empirical one.* But the similarity ends here. Unlike the Buddhist, Sartre does not think that the empirical ego can give rise to suffering. Such an ego which is *outside* consciousness cannot be the cause of the suffering of consciousness because consciousness is without cause. The ego can appear as the motive of action and thereby as a cause of suffering only in the light of a project of consciousness. Otherwise the ego is neutral. The Buddhist differs from Sartre in this respect because the former thinks that consciousness is not without cause and that the empirical ego, which is a psychic factor *(cetasika)* within consciousness, can affect the condition of consciousness.

## THE PHENOMENOLOGICAL DESCRIPTION AND VIPASSANĀ

Sartre and the Buddhist, however, give similar reasons for rejecting the permanent self. They deny the existence of the self because they cannot find it among the data given immediately to their experience. Employing the method called phenomenological description, Sartre discovers only consciousness and self-consciousness and none of them is the transcendental ego or bears reference to it.[4] The Buddhist, using the method called *vipassanā* meditation, finds only five selfless aggregates; there is no self inside or outside them.[5] In this respect, Sartre and the Buddhist are *empiricists* for the reason that they depend on the empirical investigation for proving the existence of the permanent self. When their investigation fails to reveal it, they conclude that no such self exists because there is no evidence for its existence. They reach the same conclusion because their methods of investigation are alike. Just as Sartre's phenomenological description aims at 'returning to things themselves,' so the Buddhist's *vipassanā* meditation enables one to 'see things as they are' *(yathābhūtaṁ pajānāti)*. The two methods have their foundation in reflective experience; that is, whereas phenomenological description is possible on the basis of pure reflection, *vipassanā* meditation is possible on the basis of wise attention (*yoniso-manasikāra*).[6] Pure reflection and wise attention are just different names of the same activity, for they refer to a kind of reflection which limits itself to what is really given. Pure reflection and wise attention are antithetical to impure reflection and unwise attention *(ayoniso-manasikāra)* respectively. Sartre and the Buddhist share the view that the empirical self is constituted by impure reflection or unwise attention which tends to assert more than it knows. They then maintain that once one practises phenomenological description or *vipassanā* meditation, one sees only impersonal consciousness; the constituted ego disappears.

Another similar feature in Sartre's and the Buddhist's methods lies in the fact that they are both *regressive* methods. Phenomenological description, when applied to the person, passes from the psychic life to the free impersonal consciousness and ends up in nothingness. In like manner, *vipassanā* meditation, when used for investigating the person, passes from the psychic life to momentary acts of consciousness and stops there. However, it does not reach nothingness. One question arises here: If the two methods are regressive, why do the final outcomes of their investigation differ? From the Sartrean viewpoint, the Buddhist does not regress far enough. To this, the Buddhist would say that Sartre has gone too far.

## EMPTINESS

Thus Sartre and the Buddhist hold different views on the inner structure of consciousness. According to Sartre, consciousness which is emptied of all egological structure is contentless; neither object nor image nor desire is in consciousness. Image for Sartre is an act of consciousness, it is consciousness of something. When we imagine a tree, it is a tree that we are imagining, not our image of a tree. In the same way, desire is not a psychic entity dwelling in consciousness; rather it is consciousness of something as desirable. Hence nothing is *contained* in consciousness. Since all being is on the side of the object, consciousness is a total emptiness or nothingness.

Although the Buddhist maintains that consciousness is not-self, he would not accept Sartre's view that consciousness is contentless. For the Buddhist, an image of the object is retained in consciousness and reproduced later by the act of recognition *(saññā)*. Furthermore, consciousness can never function in utter isolation; it always arises together with a number of psychic factors *(cetasika)*. Desire, for example, is a psychic factor dwelling in consciousness. Consciousness desires an object because it contains desire. The *Arahant* has no desire for any object as his consciousness is emptied of desire. Thus consciousness in Buddhism is not contentless because it contains images and psychic factors. And in so far as it contains these psychic entities, consciousness cannot be regarded as a total emptiness or nothingness. It is "consciousness-and-something-more."

## SELF-CONSCIOUSNESS

In spite of this disagreement, the Buddhist would agree with Sartre's view that consciousness is consciousness of something. The Buddhist says that consciousness is consciousness of the object *(ārammaṇaṁ cintetīti cittaṁ)*. In Buddhism the relation between consciousness and its object is called *phassa* (contact). This *phassa* is likened to the notion of intentionality in phenomenology. The Buddhist thinks that consciousness has contact with its object through one of six sense organs *(dvāra)*, viz. eye, ear, nose, tongue, body and mind. Here mind-door *(manodvāra)* is the "sixth" sense which has all mental phenomena as its objects. Consciousness can reflect upon itself and its psychic factors through this sixth sense. Without the mind-door, consciousness cannot know itself, just as a person without eye-door *(cakkhudvāra)* cannot see a visible object. Through the mind-door consciousness knows itself as an object, not as a subject. That is consciousness by nature is not self-conscious, it is not implicitly aware of itself as awareness of the object. This means that consciousness in Buddhism lacks self-transparency which is regarded as the essential characteristic of the Sartrean consciousness. In this respect, the Buddhist's viewpoint is diametrically opposed to Sartre's.

According to Sartre, self-consciousness is the "mode of existence" of consciousness; that is, consciousness exists only to the extent that it appears to itself in the mode of self-consciousness. From this it follows that self-consciousness is the necessary condition of the existence of consciousness. Consciousness, therefore, is necessarily self-conscious; that is, consciousness is implicitly aware of itself as awareness of the object. This self-consciousness precludes an unconscious consciousness. Hence the Buddhist notion of subconsciousness *(bhavaṅga-viññāṇa)* has no place in Sartre's model of consciousness.

Thus the point on which there is a major discrepancy between Sartre and the Buddhist on the inner structure of consciousness is this: whereas for Sartre consciousness is consciousness of something *plus* self-consciousness, for the Buddhist consciousness is consciousness of something *sans* self-consciousness. Since the two views are contraries, they cannot both be true. Whose view is right ? It is not easy to decide whether consciousness is self-conscious. In Western philosophy some thinkers like Descartes and Kant think that consciousness is self-conscious whereas Spinoza, Prichard and Jaakko Hintikka think otherwise. In Indian philosophy the Advaita Vedānta, the Prabhākara school of Pūrva Mimāṁsā and also the Sāṅkhya-Yoga school advocate the view that consciousness is self-conscious or self-luminous *(svaprakāśa)*. This view is rejected by the Nyāya.[7] Even the Buddhists cannot find agreement among themselves on this issue. Whereas the early Buddhist and the Mādhyamika maintain that consciousness is not self-conscious, the Vijñāṇavādin holds the view that consciousness is self-conscious. All this shows that the problem of self-consciousness is indeed a perennial philosophical problem.

The notion of consciousness as self-conscious is a vital one for Sartre's ontology, for if consciousness is not accepted as necessarily self-conscious, then it would follow that consciousness cannot be implicitly aware of itself as *not being* the object, which would imply that consciousness is not nothingness. For Sartre consciousness is a negation of being because, when it is aware of something, consciousness is aware of itself as not-being-this-thing. To support his view, Sartre cites an example:[8] I count the cigarettes which are in the case: they are a dozen. It is very possible that I have no positional consciousness of counting them. If anyone should ask me, "what are you doing there?" I should reply at once that I am counting. This reply, says Sartre, aims not only at the immediately preceding consciousness which I can know by reflection but also at those fleeting consciousnesses which have passed without being reflected on. The fact that I can recall my counting cigarettes proves that I have continuous nonpositional awareness of counting. From this it follows that consciousness is self-conscious. The early Buddhist would argue that the fact of recollection here does not necessarily confirm the existence of self-consciousness. From the Buddhist viewpoint, each consciousness, on passing away, transmits its potentialities to its immediate successor. The present consciousness is born an owner of potentialities belonging to all predecessors. And this explains how we can recall our conscious acts of counting cigarettes. Each counting consciousness, on passing away, transmits its potentialities to its successor. Recollection is possible on the basis of this continuity. No self-consciousness is involved here.

The Buddhist's argument sounds philosophically tenable to those who believe in the causal relations between two consciousnesses. But it would be unacceptable to Sartre who rejects such causal relations. It may be added here that the Buddhist differs from Sartre on the issue of self-consciousness because the former believes in the existence of the sixth sense, i.e. mind-door. As we have seen, the Buddhist maintains that consciousness knows itself only through the mind-door. As such, consciousness can know itself always as an object, never as a subject. Since one consciousness can never know two objects at one time, it is impossible for consciousness to be conscious of itself when it is conscious of an object. From Sartre's viewpoint, the Buddhist seems to have confused self-consciousness with the reflective consciousness. In reflection, consciousness is aware of its predecessor as an object. The reflective consciousness, therefore, posits an object, but in its case the object is another act of consciousness. Here reflection is knowledge because there is a certain subject-object division. But self-consciousness is not knowledge, for consciousness is aware of itself as a subject. Self-awareness, says Sartre, is "an immediate, non-cognitive relation" of consciousness to itself. Thus self-consciousness and knowledge of the reflected consciousness are "two radically different phenomena."[9] Sartre would agree with the Buddhist view that one consciousness can posit one object at one time. Sartre, however, would add that when consciousness posits an object, it always has non-positional awareness of itself as being aware of the object. Each consciousness has this basic structure: *awareness of an object and implicit awareness of being aware of the object*. To our mind, Sartre's elucidation sounds plausible. However, the early Buddhist would find it difficult to accept the

Sartrean viewpoint because he believes in the existence of the mind-door. Brushing away the notion of the mind-door, the Vijñāṇavādin of Mahāyāna Buddhism regards consciousness as self-conscious.

## THE BEING OF THE OBJECT

According to Sartre, consciousness is consciousness of something. If consciousness had nothing to be posited as its object, then it would become absolute nothingness; it would not exist as a "pure appearance." Thus the appearance of consciousness presupposes the existence of the object. This indicates that the existence of the object is the "constitutive structure" of consciousness; that is, consciousness is born supported by the object which exists in itself. Since Sartre holds the view that the object has existence independent of consciousness, he may be regarded as a realist. That Sartre's philosophy is realist can be gathered from the following statement by Sartre: "What was very important to me was realism, in other words, the idea that the world existed as I saw it and that objects I perceived were real."[10]

Like Sartre, the Buddhist thinks that consciousness is consciousness of an object. Consciousness cannot arise without causes. Since the object is a necessary cause for the arising of consciousness, consciousness cannot arise without the object. Consciousness in Buddhism is born supported by the existence of the object. The Buddhist is also a realist because he holds that the material object (*rūpa*) is non-mental and independent of consciousness. The Buddhist, however, differs from Sartre on the question of the existence of the object. For Sartre the existence of the object or being-in-itself is wholly independent or *Selbständig*, it is a full positivity which is permanent and non-temporal. For the Buddhist the existence of objects is interdependent (*paṭiccasamuppanna*); nothing exists in itself. The object is in a state of perpetual flux or flow (*santati*); hence it is impermanent and temporal. This means that there is no being-in-itself in Buddhism. The object has neither being nor non-being; rather it is a becoming (*bhava*). The Buddhist thinks that to accept either being or non-being amounts to holding an extreme view: "Everything *is*; this, Kaccāna, is one extreme view. Everything *is not*; this the second extreme view. Avoiding both these extremes, the *Tathāgata* teaches a doctrine by the middle path."[11] And what is accepted as the middle path in this connection is the concept of becoming which, according to Hegel, is a synthesis of being and non-being. Thus we agree with T.W. Rhys Davids' remarks: "According to the Buddhist, there is no Being, there is only a *Becoming*."[12]

## NOTHINGNESS AND SUÑÑATĀ

In Sartre's philosophy consciousness or being-for-itself is described as a lack or total emptiness. What consciousness lacks is the being of the object. Consciousness, therefore, is nothingness. In Buddhism, on the contrary, consciousness is not nothingness. When consciousness is described as 'void' or 'empty' (*suñña*), the term '*suñña*' is used as a synonym for *anattā* (not-self). Hence consciousness is empty because it is "empty of a self and anything belonging to a self," not because it is a lack of the being of the object. Consciousness and the object have the same type of existence, i.e. instantaneous being. They arise and perish in every moment; in brief, they are momentary (*khaṇika*). A moment of consciousness, however, is much shorter than that of the object as seventeen conscious moments are equal to one moment of an object. The rapid succession of moments of consciousness constitutes the 'stream of consciousness' (*viññāṇasota*) which flows on uninterruptedly.

## MOMENTARINESS

Although Sartre would reject the Buddhist's contention that the being of the object is instantaneous, he would agree with the latter's view that consciousness is momentary. In fact, Sartre advocated the instantaneous conception of consciousness in *The Transcendence of the Ego,* in which he maintains that consciousness is instantaneous or momentary and that the instants of consciousness succeed one another, forming the "stream of consciousness." It should be noted that Sartre, like the Buddhist, uses the term 'stream of consciousness' to describe the continual flux of conscious acts. He then faces the same problem which the Buddhist tries to solve: If consciousness is momentary or instantaneous, what unifies the discrete moments of consciousness in such a way that they constitute the self-same stream of experience? Having rejected the permanent self, Sartre and the Buddhist can never admit that the unification is effected by a permanent entity dwelling in consciousness. They categorically assert that it is consciousness that unifies itself. How can consciousness unify itself? To this question, Sartre and the Buddhist give different answers.

## THE UNITY OF CONSCIOUSNESS

In *The Transcendence of the Ego,* Sartre says that consciousness unifies itself "by a play of transversal intentionalities." By this he means that each instant of consciousness has intentional reference to its predecessor and successor by acts of retention and protention. This is to say that the present consciousness is modified by the retention of the 'just past' consciousness and the protention of the anticipated consciousness.[13] Sartre, however, does not think that the acts of retention and protention can be taken as causal relations. For Sartre, each instant of consciousness is spontaneous or self-caused; there is no causal relation between any two instants. As Sartre himself says: "Between two consciousnesses there is no cause and effect relationship ... One consciousness is not the cause of another."[14] In this respect, Sartre's position is diametrically opposed to that of the Buddhist who says that "apart from conditions, there is no arising of consciousness."[15] The Buddhist maintains that the unity of consciousness is effected by causal relations; that is, two consecutive moments of consciousness are causally related by way of contiguity *(anantara-),* immediacy *(samanantara-)* absence *(natthi-)* and disappearance *(vigata-paccaya).*[16] The effect of the four causal relations is similar to that of Sartre's *transversal intentionalities*. In Buddhism each moment of consciousness is subdivided into three submoments, namely, genesis *(uppāda)*, development *(ṭhiti)* and dissolution *(bhaṅga)*. At the submoment of genesis, consciousness is generated by potentialities belonging to the "just past" consciousness; this is a 'retention' of the past. At the sub-moment of dissolution, the present consciousness, on passing away, transmits all the potentialities to its immediate successor; this is a 'protention' into the future. The Buddhist regards the act of transmission as a causal relation. This view would be unacceptable to Sartre.

Having rejected causal relations between consciousnesses, Sartre, in *Being and Nothingness*, finds it impossible to establish even the 'slightest connection' between two instants of consciousness. In his opinion, an instant exists in the self-inclusion of identity as a being-in-itself. In Sartre's ontology the in-itself is an isolated being which does not admit any forms of relation. As such, the relation between instants which are in-itselfs is inconceivable. Facing this difficulty, Sartre, in *Being and Nothingness*, abandons the instantaneous conception of consciousness, substituting for it the conception of consciousness as *ekstatic unity*. In that work consciousness is not instantaneous; rather it is continuous. "There has been no break in continuity within the flux of the temporal development."[17] Here the question as to what unifies consciousness does not arise. This is because the ekstatic unity is the inner structure of consciousness. Consciousness does not exist first as a discrete instant in order to be unified afterwards; consciousness is always already an ekstatic unity which simultaneously exists in the three dimensions of past, present and future.

It is interesting to note here that the Buddhist who adheres to the theory of momentariness does not face the difficulty that makes Sartre disown the theory of instantaneousness of consciousness. Why is it so? This is because Sartre and the Buddhist hold different views on the ontological status of the instant of consciousness. Sartre, following Hume, thinks that each instant of consciousness is a "distinct existence"; it is a being-in-itself. He, therefore, fails to establish the relation between the instants.

The Buddhist, on the contrary, does not grant the status of 'distinct existence' to an instant of consciousness. Each instant of consciousness is "dependently originated"; therefore, it cannot exist in itself. Having no independent existence, the instant is not a being-in-itself, to use Sartre's terminology; rather it is a becoming. Thus, in its fundamental structure, the instant of consciousness cannot exist in isolation; it is causally related to its predecessor and successor. Each instant is a part of a whole process. Considered outside the process, the instant is a mere abstraction; it has no existence in its own right.

## TEMPORALITY

As mentioned above, the Sartrean consciousness is an ekstatic unity of the past, present and future. This means that consciousness is temporal; that is, temporality is the infra-structure of consciousness. Consciousness is aware of its original temporality in the mode of self-consciousness.[18] In Buddhism consciousness is said to be temporal in the sense of being impermanent *(anicca)*. For the Buddhist, time is not the original structure of consciousness; rather it is a concept *(paññatti)* which is constituted by our awareness of the rapid succession of events.[19] Thus it is on the basis of reflection upon the rapid succession of conscious moments that temporality arises. This temporality in Buddhism may be likened to Sartre's psychic temporality.[20]

## SUBCONSCIOUSNESS

So far we have considered how Sartre and the Buddhist account for the unity and continuity of consciousness. But their explanations cover only the waking state of consciousness. There remains the problem of the continuity of consciousness during dreamless sleep or *suṣupti*. Does the stream of consciousness stop flowing when man is in deep sleep? This question cannot be answered in Sartre's framework. Sartre's method of phenomenological description is based on reflective experience. Since there is no experience to be reflected upon in dreamless sleep, Sartre's method does not entitle him to deal with the question as to what becomes of consciousness when man is in deep sleep. The Buddhist's method of *vipassanā* meditation cannot do better, for it has the same limitation. The Buddhist, however, tries to answer the above question, though he cannot provide empirical evidence. He says that consciousness of a man who is in dreamless sleep continues to flow in the state of *bhavaṅga*. The Buddhist thus develops the theory of *bhavaṅga-viññāṇa* or subconsciousness. Subconsciousness is the 'process-freed' *(vīthimutta)* consciousness which cannot be known by reflection because it is under the "threshold of consciousness."[21] Although its existence cannot be proved by experience, it is postulated by the Buddhist in order to justify the continuity of consciousness during dreamless sleep. Sartre would reject the Buddhist's notion of subconsciousness for the same reason that makes him reject Husserl's doctrine of the transcendental ego; that is, subconsciousness cannot be found among the data of reflective experience. Taking into account only what is given immediately to his experience, Sartre would have to reject the Buddhist's notion of subconsciousness. The Buddhist, however, finds it necessary to introduce the conception of subconsciousness if he wants to justify not only the continuity of consciousness during dreamless sleep but also the theory of *karma* and rebirth.

## KARMA AND REBIRTH

According to the Upaniṣadic thinkers, *ātman* is immortal; it is reborn into a new life after the dissolution of the body. In spite of rejecting *ātman*, the Buddhist retains the Upaniṣadic theory of rebirth. If there is no immortal self, what then is reborn into the next life? For the Buddhist, it is consciousness which is reborn in the subconscious state. He makes it clear that it is not one and the same consciousness that transmigrates from one life to another life. The death-consciousness *(cuti-citta)* in the preceding life perishes, immediately giving birth to the rebirth-consciousness *(paṭisandhi-citta)* in the succeeding life. The two consciousnesses are "neither the same nor different," though they are essentially of the nature of subconsciousness.[22] In this way, the Buddhist claims to have avoided the two extremes, namely, eternalism and annihilationism. The Buddhist is not eternalist because he rejects the permanent self. Neither is he annihilationist because he believes in rebirth.

Having rejected the permanent self, Sartre is not an eternalist. But from the Buddhist's viewpoint Sartre is annihilationist because he does not believe in rebirth. Death for Sartre is "the nihilation of all my possibilities,"[23] hence rebirth of consciousness after death is impossible. Each life is complete in itself; it is "a unique life—that is, a life which does not begin again, a life in which one never recovers his stroke."[24] Sartre assumes that there is no rebirth because he cannot find a reason for it. He writes: "It is absurd that we are born; it is absurd that we die."[25] According to Sartre, how consciousness is born from a particular embryo is a metaphysical problem; "and this problem is perhaps insoluble."[26] Here the Buddhist would disagree with Sartre. For the Buddhist, man is born owing to his *karma*; that is the rebirth-consciousness is caused and conditioned by the Reproductive *karma* (*Janaka-kamma*). The *Arahant* whose *karma*-energy is exhausted is not reborn after death. This suggests that the Buddhist theory of rebirth is closely connected with the doctrine of *karma*.

In Buddhism *karma* or action is defined by *cetanā* or intention. By intention the Buddhist understands the self-centred, goal-directed and result-oriented volitional disposition of the ordinary person (*puthujjana*). The Buddhist takes intention to be the determinant of human actions, especially bodily and verbal actions: "Having intended, one does action by body, speech and mind."[27] This statement clearly establishes that there is a temporal distinction or time lapse between intention and action. Action is not free because it is causally produced by intention which is determined by greed (*lobha*), hatred (*dosa*) and delusion (*moha*)—the threefold root (*mūla*) of unwholesome action. The action which is done out of the threefold defilement is stored up in subconsciousness and produces result in the future. "Threefold, however, is the result of karma: ripening during this life-time, ripening in the next birth, ripening in later births."[28] Hence man's present condition is determined by his past *karma*. What he is accords with what he did; that is, man is 'heir to his action' (*kamma-dāyāda*).

Like the Buddhist, Sartre defines action by intention. What he means by intention is "a choice of the end."[29] Sartre seems to deny any time lapse between forming an intention and actually acting. Thus to make a choice of the end is to act. As such, intention is not a cause of action; it is action itself. For Sartre action is free because the end that one chooses is in the future; hence it cannot be thought of as an occurrence that precedes and causally brings about the action. Now it is clear that Sartre's action theory is different from that of the Buddhist. Whereas the Buddhist holds that human action is to be understood as causally produced by antecedent conditions in the agent's consciousness, Sartre thinks that human action can be explained only in a teleological fashion, that is, by appeal to the agent's end or goal which cannot be regarded as causally related to action. In Buddhism action is not free because it is determined and motivated by the three motives, namely, greed, hatred and delusion, but in Sartre's philosophy action is free because the so-called motives are outside consciousness and have meaning only within the compass of the project towards the end.[30]

Sartre, however, would agree with the Buddhist view that man is what he makes of himself. For Sartre man is defined by his action: "he is therefore nothing else but the sum of his actions."[31] What man has done in the past is his "essence"; it is what it is. Here we come across another difference between the Buddhist and Sartre. According to the Buddhist, essence precedes existence; that is, man's past *karma* determines and conditions his present existence. But, for Sartre, existence precedes essence; that is, man's past action is surpassed by his present existence, at the present human reality is not what it is. This means that for Sartre the past action, being cut off from the present by self-consciousness, does not determine man's present condition. What man has done lapses into the past without the possibility of producing a result in the future. Hence the Buddhist's view on the retribution of action is unacceptable to Sartre. The Buddhist holds that human action is accumulated by consciousness and transmitted to its successor through causal relations. And by this process *karma*-energy is transmitted from one consciousness to another. The present consciousness is born an owner of the past karma and experiences its fruit which ripens at that moment. This retribution of *karma* presupposes the cause-effect relationship between consciousnesses. Since Sartre has rejected such relationship, he has ruled out the possibility of the retribution of action in his philosophy.

## FREEDOM

Sartre would not accept the Buddhist view about the cause-effect relationship between consciousnesses because this view is against his own notion of freedom. According to Sartre, consciousness is free as it is spontaneous or self-caused. That each consciousness has causal independence is proved by the fact that when consciousness posits its immediate predecessor as its object, it is aware of itself as not being the reflected consciousness. For Sartre this reflective separation entails the suspension of causality. Here Sartre's position is not tenable as *he seems to confuse psychological negation with causal independence.* Psychological negation is an insufficient premise from which one can draw a conclusion for causal independence. The mere fact that consciousness is implicitly aware of itself as not being its immediate predecessor does not prove that the two consciousnesses have no causal relation. Sartre's phenomenological description entitles him to describe an aspect of consciousness as it appears to reflection. As such, the method excludes the notion of "cause" which is in principle "prior" to the appearance of consciousness. Since the method is a description of "what appears," a causal investigation is *a priori* impossible.

Nevertheless the view that consciousness is self-caused or

spontaneous is vital for Sartre's notion of freedom. Consciousness is free because it is not causally related to anything. This causal independence enables consciousness to wrench itself away from the object, to break off with its own past and to tear itself away from what it will be in the future. Here Sartre uses the term 'freedom' as a synonym for spontaneity or uncaused origination. This type of freedom is the inner structure of consciousness and may be characterized as *ontological freedom.* In this respect, the Buddhist view is rather different from Sartre's. For the Buddhist, consciousness is dependently originated; it is not spontaneous or self-caused. The conception of spontaneous consciousness is not acceptable to the Buddhist because it is incompatible with the law of Dependent Origination (*paṭiccasamuppāda*). Thus if by freedom one means uncaused origination, then consciousness in Buddhism is not free.

## FREEDOM FROM DESIRE

Sartre also uses the term freedom in the sense of 'undetermined choice.' For Sartre consciousness and choice are one and the same thing. Consciousness is free as its intention or choice of the end is determined neither by causes nor by motives. Sartre says that causes and motives, far from determining the choice, appear only in the light of the project towards the end.[32] Here freedom of choice may be characterized as *psychological freedom.* As we have seen, in Buddhism the ordinary person *(puthujjana)* has no such freedom because his intention *(cetanā) is* determined by desire *(taṇhā)* which manifests itself in the forms of the threefold root of action, namely, greed, hatred and delusion. The ordinary person, however, can gradually liberate himself by getting rid of desire. And his freedom is present in inverse proportion to desire; the less desire he has in his consciousness, the more freedom he obtains. Man has absolute freedom only when he attains *Nirvāṇa* which is described as *"freedom from desire."*[33] For the Buddhist, only the consciousness of a liberated person (*Arahant*) is free because it is totally emptied of desire.

It is worth noting that the Buddhist, unlike Sartre, does not look upon freedom as the inner structure of consciousness. In contrast with Sartre's statement that consciousness is freedom, the Buddhist would rather say that consciousness is born without freedom, but it can become free. In Buddhism consciousness becomes free only when it realizes *Nirvāṇa*. This view is different from that of Sartre who says that "man does not exist first in order to be free subsequently, there is no difference between the being of man and his being free."[34] For the Buddhist, man is born without freedom because at that moment his consciousness is full of desire. Man can obtain freedom when desire is eliminated from his consciousness. Hence freedom is incompatible with desire. There is no such incompatibility in Sartre's notion of freedom. According to Sartre, consciousness is free as its original choice is free. Consciousness chooses because it is a desire to be the in-itself which it lacks. Without desire, consciousness would stop choosing and freedom would be meaningless. For freedom to be meaningful, consciousness has to exercise its choice, and to make a choice, consciousness must have the desire to be. From this it follows that *freedom cannot be separated from desire*. Since Sartre defines desire as "a lack of being"[35] and takes freedom to be "synonymous with lack,"[36] it is quite legitimate to assume that desire and freedom are one and the same thing.

Thus, unlike Sartre who holds the view that freedom is not incompatible with desire, the Buddhist maintains that *freedom is freedom from desire*. From the Buddhist viewpoint the Sartrean consciousness is not absolutely free for the reason that it is determined, by desire, to choose the ideal, i.e. the being-in-itself-for-itself. Every free choice presupposes alternatives, but in the case of the ideal there is no alternative. Hence consciousness is not free not to choose its ultimate goal, though it is free to choose the means thereto. The Buddhist thinks that so far as man has to choose under compulsion of desire, he is doomed to frustration and suffering. Desire, therefore, is the cause of suffering. As stated in the *Mahāsatipaṭṭhāna-Sutta:* "What, now, is the Noble Truth of the Origin of Suffering? It is *desire (taṇhā)* which gives rise to fresh rebirth, and, bound up with pleasure and lust, now here, now there, finds ever fresh delight."[37] To overcome suffering, one has to destroy its cause, i.e., desire. Once desire is eliminated from consciousness, one realizes *Nirvāṇa* which is sometimes described as "freedom from all suffering" (*sabbadukkhapamocana*).[38]

## FREEDOM FROM SUFFERING

Sartre would agree with the Buddhist view that desire gives rise to suffering. Consciousness, as the desire to be, has a permanent attention towards an identification with the being of the object. Such an identification is impossible because all identification with the being-in-itself requires the disappearance of consciousness.[39] As such, it is an ideal that can never be realized by consciousness. As consciousness always desires to realize this unrealizable ideal, it is regarded as a "useless passion." And this passion is a constant cause of frustration and suffering. It is not possible for man to overcome this suffering because his desire for the ideal is neither satiable nor destructible. For Sartre desire cannot be eliminated from consciousness because it is the inner structure of consciousness. The elimination of desire would require the disappearance of consciousness. Since consciousness always has desire, it is subject to suffering for ever. *The complete cessation of suffering is impossible in Sartre's philosophy*. That is why Sartre says that so long as consciousness appears in the world, it is "by nature an unhappy consciousness with no possibility of surpassing its unhappy state."[40]

Here the Buddhist is rather different. He believes that it is possible for consciousness to surpass its unhappy state. Consciousness will be free from all suffering if desire is eliminated: "What, monks, is the Noble Truth of the Cessation of Suffering? It is the complete fading away and extinction of this desire."[41] In this respect, the Buddhist's difference from Sartre is due to the fact that for the former desire is destructible whereas for the latter it is not. In Buddhism desire is regarded, not as the inner structure of consciousness, but as one of the unwholesome psychic factors *(akusala-cetasika)* which can be found only in unwholesome consciousness. Since desire is not present in all kinds of consciousness, it is legitimate to assume that some consciousness exists without desire. For instance, the *Arahant's* consciousness is emptied of desire. It follows that the elimination of desire does not require the disappearance of consciousness. Only suffering is overcome when its cause, desire, is destroyed. Thus *Nirvāṇa* or freedom from suffering is a realizable ideal in Buddhism. The ultimate goal of the Buddhist religious life is the attainment of *Nirvāṇa.*

> *"The purpose of the religious life does not consist in acquiring alms, honour, or fame, nor in gaining morality, concentration, or the eye of knowledge. That which is unshakeable freedom of mind, this is the goal of the religious life, this the pith, this the culmination."*[42]

## THE BUDDHIST AND SARTREAN ETHICS

According to the Buddhist, *Nirvāṇa* is attainable not only in theory but also in practice. To attain *Nirvāṇa,* one has to follow the way of life conducive to the cessation of suffering (*dukkhanirodhagaminīpaṭipadā*). This way of life is governed by the standards of moral conduct generally regarded as Buddhist ethics. It is known as the "Middle Path" (*Majjhimā-paṭipadā*) because it avoids two extremes: indulgence in sensual pleasure (*kāmasukhallikānuyoga*) and self-mortification (*attakilamathānuyoga*).[43] This Middle Path is referred to as the Noble Eightfold Path (*Ariya-aṭṭhaṅgikamagga*) because it is composed of eight factors, namely:

| | | |
|---|---|---|
| 1. | Right Understanding | *Sammā-diṭṭhi* |
| 2. | Right Thought | *Sammā-saṅkappa* |
| 3. | Right Speech | *Sammā-vācā* |
| 4. | Right Action | *Sammā-kammanta* |
| 5. | Right Livelihood | *Sammā-ājīva* |
| 6. | Right Effort | *Sammā-vāyāma* |
| 7. | Right Mindfulness | *Sammā-sati* |
| 8. | Right Concentration | *Sammā-samādhi* |

The figurative expression 'path' (*magga*) should not mislead us into thinking that the single factors have to be followed and practised one after the other in numerical order as in the list above. In practice, factors three to five, which form the section of 'morality' (*sīla*), have to be perfected first. Morality is the intention present in one who abstains from killing, stealing, etc., or in one who fulfils the observances.[44] To develop moral habit, one has to observe various rules of conduct prescribed by the Buddha. Having acquired moral habit, one is capable of practising factors six to eight, which constitute the section of 'concentration' (*samādhi*). The three factors form parts of the Buddhist method known as 'concentration meditation' (*samatha-bhāvanā*). After that preparation, one is capable of practising the first two factors forming the section of 'wisdom' (*paññā*). This Buddhist method called 'insight meditation' (*vipassanā-bhāvanā*) aims at developing Right Understanding and Right Thought.

Now it is clear that in the Buddhist ethics *Nirvāṇa* or freedom (*vimutti*) is the ultimate goal and the Middle Path, consisting of morality, concentration and wisdom, the means for reaching the goal. Prescribed rules of conduct have to be observed by the aspirant for freedom. The rules bid one perform action conducive to freedom. Once freedom is obtained, the rules may be discarded. Just as a man abandons a raft after using it to cross a river, so also the liberated person gives up *dhamma* after attaining *Nirvāṇa;* he is beyond good and evil:

> *"I have taught a doctrine similar to a raft—it is for crossing over, not for carrying. You, monks, who understand that the teaching is similar to a raft, should give up even good things (dhamma); how much more so then should you give up evil things (adhamma)."* [45]

In the Sartrean ethics, freedom is the goal of human action; it is the end in itself, for Sartre declares that "freedom, in respect of concrete circumstances, can have no other end and aim but itself."[46] The actions of a man of good faith have the quest of freedom as their ultimate significance. In Sartre's ethics, however, there is no prescribed means or *magga* for bringing about the end. This is because Sartre, unlike the Buddhist, takes freedom to be the inner structure of consciousness. Although man is always already free, he hides freedom from himself by putting himself in bad faith. To liberate his being, man need not observe any rules of conduct. *What is required for escaping bad faith is the realization that one is free.* For Sartre, to follow any prescribed rules of conduct involves bad faith, for they enable man to escape the existential burden of free choice. Hence the so-called 'prescribed morality' (*paññatti-sīla*) in the Buddhist ethics has no place in Sartre's ethics.

## THE RADICAL CONVERSION

In spite of all this, we find what is similar to the last section of the Buddhist 'Path' in Sartre's ethics. That is, the Buddhist thinks that wisdom (*paññā*) which realizes *Nirvāṇa* has to be developed by practising insight meditation. Sartre likewise maintains that man can escape bad faith by *purifying reflection.*[47] A man of bad faith refuses to recognize what he really is, namely, *a being who is both facticity and transcendence.*[48] He tries to forget that his past or facticity is always already surpassed by his future-oriented choice, seeking either to maintain or revive the past. His impure reflection which is in bad faith constitutes the empirical self out of past conscious acts and mistakes it for his true being. Identifying his being with the empirical self, the man of bad faith takes root in the world.

> *"He does not even imagine any longer the possibility of getting out of the world, for he has given to himself the type of existence of the rock, the consistency, the inertia, the capacity of being-in-the-midst-of-the-world."*[49]

He thus has a 'wrong view' (*micchādiṭṭhi*), to use Buddhist terminology. His "deliverance and salvation" can be achieved only after a *"radical conversion."*[50] Since bad faith is a refusal to recognize one's true being, deliverance from bad faith requires the recognition of that being. This recognition would result in "a self-recovery of being which was previously corrupted."[51]

The self-recovery Sartre calls *authenticity* or *good faith*. How can man recognize his true being ? It is through pure reflection that man recognizes what he really is. Through it he realizes that the meaning of the world and values have their origin in his own intentionality. Having realized this, he lives in the world with the spirit of play.

Sartre, therefore, says that "play ... releases subjectivity." Through it man himself sets the value and rules for his acts and consents to play only according to the rules which he himself has established and defined. "As a result, there is in a sense 'little reality' in the world."[52] Through the spirit of play man approaches the world as a playground, having no attachment to it; he, therefore, "could not be concerned with *possessing* a being in the world."[53] He takes the world symbolically and playfully, not appropriately and seriously. He lets the earth support him, but does not succumb to the illusion that he can acquire its *permanence*. Consequently he liberates himself from the motive of the desire to be the being-in-itself-for-itself. According to J.P. Fell, "this will mean, to those familiar with *L'Être el le Néant*, that Sartre is calling for *a radical conversion that delivers one from the metaphysical quest for an ideal being*."[54]

Thus the radical conversion consists in a change from a life in bad faith to a life of authenticity. This radical change affects not only man's attitude towards the world but also his way of life. He lives in the world with the *spirit of detachment*. We find something similar to Sartre's notion of radical conversion in Buddhism where the ordinary person (*puthujjana*) is said to be transformed into the *Arahant* or liberated person. Seeing the true nature of things, the *Arahant* has a new attitude towards life; his picture of the world (*papañca*) has been destroyed. Finding no "reality" in the world, he has no desire to possess anything. *The Arahant, like Sartre's man of good faith, lives in the world with the spirit of detachment*:

> *"Not constituting, not thinking out for being or for non-being, he grasps after nothing in the world; not grasping, he is not troubled; being untroubled, he himself attains Nirvāṇa."*[55]

## CONCLUSION

The conclusion which we can draw from the foregoing comparisons is that for both Sartre and the Buddhist consciousness is emptied of the permanent self. Being aware of its emptiness, consciousness has the desire to be something that it is not. To fulfill its desire *(taṇhā)*, consciousness constitutes the empirical self through impure reflection or unwise attention *(ayoniso-manasikāra)*.

According to Sartre, consciousness identifies its true being with the empirical self and thereby takes root in the world. Forgetting that it is by nature an impersonal spontaneity, consciousness is in bad faith *(mauvaise foi)*. Consciousness, however, can liberate itself from bad faith and establish itself in good faith through pure reflection and the spirit of play.

According to the Buddhist, consciousness clings to the empirical self (*attavādupādāna*) and thereby loses itself in the world; it is in the state of ignorance (*avijjā*). Nevertheless consciousness can free itself from ignorance through the wise attention *(yoniso-manasikāra)* of insight meditation *(vipassanā-bhāvanā)*. Hence the Buddhist, like Sartre, grants the highest value to freedom of consciousness. The life which is worth living is the life of freedom or *vimutti*. Man can live with freedom after a radical conversion.

Thus Sartre and the Buddhist alike believe in the possibility of the radical conversion that results in the deliverance of consciousness from the phenomenal world *(papañca)*, the meaning of which is constituted by consciousness itself. *And it is this belief in the radical conversion that brings Sartre's existentialism closest to early Buddhism.*

## NOTES

1 See above. pp. 100-103.
2 Cf. S. IV. 384: "Both formerly and now also, Anurādha, it is just suffering and the cessation of suffering that I proclaim."
3 See above, pp. 37, 116.

4 See above, pp. 32-33.
5 See above, pp. 107-111.
6 See above, pp. 117-119.
7 Saksena, S.K., *Nature of Consciousness in Hindu Philosophy*, Motilal Banarsidass, Delhi, 1971, pp. 72, 77.
8 BN. 13.
9 Sartre, J-P., "Consciousness of Self and Knowledge of Self," in N. Lawrence and D. O'Connor (ed.), *Readings in Existential Phenomenology*, Prentice-Hall Inc., 1967, p. 122.
10 "Interview with Jean-Paul Sartre", in P.A. Schilpp (ed.), *The Philosophy of Jean-Paul Sartre*, Open Court, 1981, p. 10.
11 S.XXII. 5.90.
12 Rhys Davids, T.W., *Early Buddhism*, Bharatiya Publishing House, 1976, p. 56.
13 S. XXXV. 85; See above, pp. 164-167.
14 TE. 69.
15 TE. 39.
16 See above, p. 30-31.
17 Sartre, J-P., *The Psychology of Imagination*, Methuen, London, 1978, p. 27.
18 M. I. 257.
19 See above, pp. 135-136.
20 BN. 63.
21 See above, pp. 58-59.
22 See above, pp. 155-157.
23 See above, pp. 155-157.
24 See above, pp. 141-143.
25 See above, pp. 145-147.
26 BN. 687.
27 BN. 674.
28 BN. 699.
29 BN. 198.
30 A. VI. 63: "Cetayitvā kammaṁ karoti kāyena vācāya manasā".
31 Ibid.
32 BN. 614.
33 See above, pp. 69-70.
34 Sartre, J-P., *Existentialism and Humanism*, tr. by Philip Mairet, Eyre Methuen, London, 1980, p. 41.
35 See above pp. 69-70.
36 MA. I. 236.
37 BN. 60.
38 BN. 735.
39 BN. 722.
40 D. II. 308.
41 S. XXI. 4.
42 See above p. 84.
43 BN. 140.

44 D. II. 310.
45 M.I. 197.
46 M. I. 197.
47 Vism. I. 6.
48 M. I. 134-5.
49 Sartre, J-P., *Existentialism and Humanism*, p. 51.
50 BN. 742.
51 See above, pp. 82-83.
52 BN. 741.
53 BN. 534n.
54 BN. 116n.
55 BN. 741.
56 Ibid.
57 Ibid.
58 Fell, J.P., *Heidegger and Sartre*, Columbia University Press, New York, 1979, p. 152.
59 M. III. 244.

# *Index*

## B

## C

## D



## E

## F



## G



## H

## I



## J



## K

## N

## V



## W



## Y